TRIGGERS

DAVID RICHO

TRIGGERS

HOW WE CAN

STOP REACTING

AND START HEALING

Shambhala
Boulder
2019

Shambhala Publications, Inc.
2129 13th Street
Boulder, Colorado 80302
www.shambhala.com

14 13 12 11 10 9 8 7 6

Printed in the United States of America

Shambhala Publications makes every effort to print on acid-free,
recycled paper.

Shambhala Publications is distributed worldwide by
Penguin Random House, Inc., and its subsidiaries.

Designed by Kate Huber-Parker

Library of Congress Cataloging-in-Publication Data
Names: Richo, David, 1940– author.
Title: Triggers: how we can stop reacting and start healing/David Richo.
Description: First edition. | Boulder: Shambala, [2019]
Identifiers: LCCN 2019007666 | ISBN 9781611807653 (paperback;
alk. paper)
Subjects: LCSH: Behavior modification. | Emotional conditioning. |
Stimulus generalization. | Emotions.
Classification: LCC BF637.B4 R53 2019 | DDC 155.9—dc23
LC record available at https://lccn.loc.gov/2019007666

For Beverly

Walking with a friend in the dark
is better than walking alone in the light.

—Helen Keller

CONTENTS

Introduction   1

ONE: WHAT TRIGGERS US AND WHY?   9
Real and Imagined Triggers   18
When the Trigger Is Inside Us   21
Inner Demons   26
What Makes Triggers So Disturbing   30

TWO: TRAUMAS AND RESOURCES   37
Childhood Wounds and Neuroscience   37
Healthy Ways to Connect Our Then and Now   39
How Much of Me Is Me?   45

THREE: HOW TO HANDLE A TRIGGER   51
Handy Tools   53
Shadow, Ego, Early Life: What's Really Going On?   59
Practices That Increase Our Personal Inner
    Resources   68

FOUR: THE SADNESS TRIGGER   79
Grief about What We Missed Early On   80
Mourning a Death   83
When Others Are Sad   85
Tears in Our Mortal Story   92

FIVE: THE ANGER TRIGGER   95
Is It Anger or Abuse?   96
The Angry Ego   100
Why We Fear Others' Anger   102
A New World   105

SIX: THE FEAR TRIGGER 111

Both Desires and Fears 113

When Closeness Is Scary 115

Practices for Freeing Ourselves from the Grip
of Fear 120

Mindfulness and Loving-Kindness for Fearlessness 122

SEVEN: RELATIONSHIP TRIGGERS AND
RESOURCES 127

True Companions 131

When Our Feelings Are Hurt 134

Difficult Patterns in Relationships 138

States of the Union 142

Danger in the Electronics Sector? 143

Practices That Increase Our Relationship
Resources 146

EIGHT: SPIRITUAL RESOURCES 153

When the Time Has Come 155

Neuroplasticity and Spirituality 157

Practices That Increase Our Spiritual Resources 159

EPILOGUE: THE FIRES THAT SHOW
AND TELL 171

Appendix: Affirmations to Free Ourselves from
the Grip of Fear 175

About the Author 181

TRIGGERS

INTRODUCTION

Someone says something to us, and we are suddenly struck with a sinking feeling in our stomach. Someone does something and instantly we become enraged or alarmed. Someone comes at us with a certain attitude and we go to pieces. We hear mention of a person, place, or thing that is associated with an unresolved issue or a past trauma and we immediately feel ourselves seize up with sadness, anger, fear, or shame. When any of this happens, we can be sure a trigger has been pulled. We find ourselves in a stimulus-response experience that happens to all of us. The stimulus is referred to in metaphorical terms, as either a "trigger" or a "button": "What she said triggered me," "What he does pushes my buttons," "I got hooked again." We might also say, "I have a charge on this," using an electrical analogy.

A trigger is any word, person, event, or experience that touches off an immediate emotional reaction—for example, sadness, depression, anger, aggression, fear, panic, or humiliation, shame. Words, behavior, attitudes, events, even the presence of certain people, can incite reflex reactions in us over which we have no control. For example, we are suddenly surprised by a noise and we are startled. The noise is the stimulus/trigger; the startle is the reaction. Our reaction can be brief or long. Sometimes we can move through our reaction in a moment. Sometimes it becomes an obsession, hard to shake off. This disempowers us and plunges us into a sense of being unsafe and insecure.

Our reaction to a trigger is often excessive, larger than what is warranted by the stimulus, longer-lasting than what fits the triggering event. The extent to which a trigger affects us is proportional to how thick- or thin-skinned we are. The more sensitive we are to others' behavior toward us, the more fiercely does our fear, anger, or shame erupt. As we become stronger, more self-assured, we notice that the arrows of others don't penetrate so deeply. In a wider context, regarding ourselves and society, we need to develop a thick enough skin to cope with our world and its shadow side rather than hide from it. Then we can face the onslaughts of our imposing world with courage to deal and heal. This book can help us do this. We can come to notice what triggers us and understand why. This is how we reclaim our power, have more choice about our immediate reactions, find healing from processing a trigger experience. When a trigger stays the night with us, lasts too long, it is a *signal*. There is something to look into, to deal with. For instance, someone at work has triggered us and it is keeping us up at night. We are finding out that we need to have a conversation with him, work the conflict out, speak up for ourselves. This is an example of how a trigger can beckon us to healthy assertiveness.

Our reaction is also based on our belief about how serious the trigger is. Examples of beliefs are assumptions, illusions, projections, suppositions. Our reaction moves from belief to expression first as a feeling and then sometimes with a follow-up of words or actions. Usually all this happens without our having a chance to consider what makes the most sense for us in the situation. Triggers and reactions happen so fast that we don't have a chance to pause, look at what is really happening, and make a wise choice. This is because triggers activate our limbic system, where the emotions reside, not our prefrontal cortex, where rational thoughts preside. We might say that the limbic system is like a horse, at times spirited, at times wild. The prefrontal cortex is like reins. We are the riders, with varying, but certainly improvable, levels of skill.

"Trigger" is an appropriate metaphor for what provokes these immediate reactions because the "gun," the catalyst of our reaction, is in the hands of someone else. Using the "button" metaphor—as in "He pushes my buttons"—suggests that someone does something and a nuclear reaction is set off in us. When the trigger is a "hook," we are pulled into a reaction we regret or are angry at ourselves for biting it again. All three metaphors show how we lose our personal power. Someone or something has hijacked our equanimity, gained power over our feelings and actions. This is why triggers exaggerate our feeling, reaction, and belief about their meaning. All this is totally normal. Being triggered is not dysfunctional, though our reaction to a trigger might be.

In my work as a therapist and teacher I have heard clients and students talk about being triggered with increasing frequency in recent years. Some trigger experiences can be quite serious—for example, a soldier with PTSD triggered by a sound that reminds him of combat, or a sexual assault survivor triggered by a touch that reminds her of her abuser. Other triggers may be connected to less-dramatic experiences, but people's reactions still seem to take control over them. This book explores all kinds of triggers and reactions. I hope it will help you find greater understanding and relief, but it is important to note that some triggers and reactions are so deeply ingrained and powerful that working with a trained therapist may be an essential step in finding healing.

A person triggers us in direct proportion to how important he has become to us in reality or in our minds. For instance, someone we care deeply about may trigger us by showing any sign of abandoning us. Someone who threatens or scares us will easily trigger us, even when he does not intend to do so. Someone we have a crush on and obsess about will trigger us by almost anything she does. When we have given power to someone, we have placed his or her finger on a trigger—and sometimes it is a hair trigger. But this does not mean that we should avoid caring about people— rather, we can learn to understand and work with our triggers and reactions.

Sometimes a trigger can be immediate, here and now, with no earlier example of it. For instance, the first time we hear of a person in our family dying, we are stricken with grief and we weep.

Usually, however, a trigger is a replay of an earlier experience. The original stimulus can be anything from a minor distress last year to a major trauma decades ago, especially in our childhood years. Those early experiences evoked grief that we have not yet fully felt or resolved. Thus, triggers can arouse post-traumatic stress that we wish to avoid. Yet, they also thereby give us a lively chance to recognize and mourn our losses, disappointments, and abuses. Indeed, every trigger is a catalyst for grief. Our sudden reaction—for example, sadness and chagrin—is how we *begin* to show that grief.

A triggering event that is a throwback to an archaic trauma feels like it is happening in the present. The brain's amygdala, part of our limbic system, stores original traumas and fear reactions with no sense of time, of impact, or of our intervening years of growth and self-strengthening. This is why triggers today can give us the sense that we are still as powerless as we were in childhood. We forget that we have inner resources to help us deal with challenges, or we neglect to use these resources because that part of the brain is not online; the amygdala has commandeered all the channels. Sometimes when we are triggered, for instance, we become mute, dumbfounded, numb. Our amygdala has silenced our thinking mind. We rebuke ourselves later as we gain back our full mental powers. We think, "I should have said . . ." But we did not have access to that calm thought process because the limbic system had blunted it. Triggers activate the sympathetic nervous system. We are moved toward flight, fight, or freeze. Stress hormones chime in, all beyond our immediate control—another reason we feel powerless.

Today, thanks to neuroscience—and more specifically, research on brain plasticity—we are aware that we can reprogram our neurological pathways to change our self-defeating patterns. The prefrontal cortex can come up with healthy ways to respond to events. Then we do not have to be at the mercy of immediate, irrational, and unplanned reactions. Yet, nonetheless, the impulse to react does not disappear easily even when we lay down new neural patterns. Our spiritual practices may also help somewhat, but not even they are always robust enough to cancel our limbic reactions entirely. So we do not have to be hard on ourselves when we still react in ways we are uncomfortable with. Instead, we can observe, learn, and practice.

Indeed, with conscious attention, our prefrontal cortex can reframe events and experiences so they do not have to be so triggering. The prefrontal cortex in full activation can calm some of the amygdala's overblown reactions. To move from our primitive brain to our "reasonable cortex" we can evoke an alternative thought that is positive and resource-enhancing. Gradually, the new thought takes over. St. Paul wrote, "Brothers and sisters, whatever is true, whatever is noble, whatever is right, whatever is pure, whatever is lovely, whatever is admirable—if anything is excellent or praiseworthy—think about such things" (Philippians 4:8).

A trigger can, of course, be positive—a stimulus arousing joy, erotic excitement, or optimism: We are triggered with chills and a lump in our throat when our team scores a win or when we see an example of the triumph of the human spirit. A photo of happy times gone by might trigger a warm sense of nostalgia. We are triggered when we experience love at first sight or feel the magic of a kiss. But today we use the word "trigger" mostly to refer to what is disturbing and unpleasant. Our topic in this book is that negative triggering—triggering that arouses not only sadness, anger, or fear but also, at times, hurt, shame, guilt, disappointment, letdown, regret, despair. In these cases, our reflex action might be fleeing, fighting, or freezing—but all overdone. Our experience feels negative when we flee too fast, fight too hard, freeze too long.

A trigger can dead-end by leading only to a reaction, with no resource that would allow us to cope with our reaction. In this book, we shall see that triggers don't have to end that way once we have tools to handle them. We can insert a third option between stimulus and response. We can move from a two-part experience to a three-part practice:

Trigger → Reaction

Can become:
Trigger → Reaction → Resource

Then, gradually, it might happen this way:
Trigger → Resource

We can mobilize inner resources not only to cope with triggering events but even to work through the traumas that caused them, to heal some of our post-traumatic stress. The triggers then have less power over us. We move from feeling unsafe to safer and from feeling insecure to more secure, the essence of self-trust. Triggers thrive on the illusion that we can't trust ourselves. With inner resources we find out we can trust ourselves indeed—and in deed.

Trauma never goes entirely away but it can become what happened rather than what still hurts. We will not eliminate triggers altogether, but we no longer have to react to them so extremely. We can modify both our susceptibility to being triggered and our reactions to being triggered. We can learn to catch ourselves before we react blindly. The impact of triggers can be blunted, and our reaction time can be shortened. We can disable the trigger mechanism so that we are not wounded, only scratched.

All this happens when we engage in serious work on our traumas, especially in therapy. We then become more aware of the connection between triggers and what we have to work on in ourselves: *Our goal is not to root out all our triggers but to find a trailhead from them into the psychological and spiritual work that has been so long awaiting us. This is how we turn our triggers into tools.*

As we marshal our inner resources, more and more of our daily triggers can turn into information with no further invasions into our peace of mind: "Oh, he said that." "Hmm, she is doing that." "Looks like they have *that* attitude toward me. How interesting." We keep in mind in all our discussions about traumas, however, that some were so serious and severe that they might not easily go away and resources may not easily kick in.

In this book, we learn how our inner resources are capacities that help us handle what we feel, what we experience, what others do to us, what happens to us, what life sends our way. A resource is a technology, a competency that we can learn to access with ease, aplomb, and swiftness. When we're triggered, we do not have to be victims of what others say or do. We are equipped to handle the "slings and arrows" that come at us. The chapters that follow will help us "take arms against a sea of troubles." Tender arms, of course.

Inner resources are like aquifers nourishing us. They help us trust that what happens will not do what triggers can do: throw us for a loop, plunge us into despondency, turn us into targets, or make us collapse in fear or shame. Our best inner resource is our natural resourcefulness, our inventiveness and ingenuity in making the most of any hand we are dealt or in dodging any bullet headed in our direction.

This does not mean that we will not sometimes have more to face than we can handle. Inner supplies can, at times, be so minimal that they cannot match the trigger or crisis that has assailed us. When that happens, we activate the inner resource that gives our immediate inadequacy a boost: We ask for help. We turn to our outer resources, our support system, to help us through.

We turn within for valuable resources, both psychological and spiritual. Psychology helps us develop inner resources like awareness of our needs and the ability to express and fulfill them in all the right places. We can learn to manage our feelings, to free ourselves from inhibition, to trust our ingenuity. Spirituality offers resources such as meditation, mindfulness, freedom from attachment, letting go of ego. Each of these can become a characteristic of our personality. Our psychological work and spiritual practices work together to increase and enrich our inner resources. Eventually we become what we practice.

The alternative responses might include turning to an addiction in the face of anxiety or threat. We might use food, sex, alcohol or other drugs to deal with the curve balls life pitches to us. All this diminishes our resourcefulness. But no matter how rusty our tools have become we can restore them to full luster. Here is the path we will find in this book: We focus first on triggers, what they are, why they happen, and where they come from. Then we look at the tools that help us handle them, both in us and around us. These resources are psychological, neuro-scientific, and spiritual. We then pay particular attention to the triggers that lead to sadness, anger, and fear. Since these are the three main feeling components of grief, we explore that dimension. We also look at how triggers happen in relationships. In all the sections, we will find useful practices, including ones from Buddhist teachings. As the reader, you may be struck by passages in this book that you highlight or underline. I recommend noting these ideas in a journal or on an iPad and pondering their meanings. You can also write them out on cards and create a set of flashcards to work with daily. What strikes any of us in a book is a positive trigger that can point to our work on ourselves. Healing in many areas of our lives is the welcome result.

Each of us can ask, "Have my inner reserves been substantial enough to accommodate the triggers and challenges in my life story so far?" What follows in these pages explores that question and constructs a compass for our journey through whatever mysterious forest we find ourselves in.

ONE

WHAT TRIGGERS US AND WHY?

In this chapter we peer more intently into our topic of triggers. We learn about ourselves and our past by what triggers us. We learn about ourselves and our feelings by our reactions. We find ways to move from autopilot to self-piloting, from reactions to responses. Our triggers then turn into sources of healing and we become enormously optimistic about our own powers of transformation.

There are no bulletproof vests for the psyche. It is a fact of life that some events have an emotional impact and activate a stressful reaction in us—they hook us, yank our chain. In fact, "trigger" is from a Dutch word meaning "pull." When we are triggered, we are pulled into a reaction. We might feel scared, lose our temper, feel hurt, be stricken with grief, be shocked, have the wind knocked out of us, fall apart.

Some events simply irk us but do not lead to an over-the-top reaction. When we simply notice a stimulus without reacting, we are not triggered. Witnessing is the opposite of being triggered. This is why mindfulness—witnessing the here and now without reacting—is an essential tool for having fewer triggers and efficiently handling the ones we have.

"He triggers me when he comes at me that way!" "She pushes my buttons as no one else can!" "They hook me every time." In all of these scenarios we may feel like victims of our triggers and of other people. In reality, triggers are tricksters. They make a two-part experience seem like one. This is because our reaction happens so close on the heels of the stimulating event. Actually, the trigger—part one of the experience—is indeed instigated by someone else. But our reaction—part two—is our own responsibility and is based on our own past experiences. We are being bullied by our own unfinished business. A triggering experience alerts us to a psychological issue in ourselves that needs to be addressed, processed, and resolved. The trigger finger is especially our own when we simply let one triggering event after another occur, especially with the same person. He or she is not the cause of the trigger, only the catalyst. A trigger arouses, evokes, or induces; it does not produce. A trigger is a contributing factor, not a determining factor. Each of us will react differently in accord with the personal issues a trigger incites, in the same way that the term "Everglades" will evince a different reaction and have a different meaning to a resident of Florida than to a resident of Kansas.

However, I also have a disclaimer: There are times when a trigger reaction *is* caused by someone. There are times when we do not have much choice about how we will react or respond. In cases of violent physical attack, for instance, we are triggered into a fearful or defensive reaction. Someone inflicting harm on our bodies is not a catalyst; he is the cause of our distress. This applies to any abuse of which we are victims.

Our feelings in reaction to triggers are on a spectrum from being caused to being catalyzed. The degree of threat or impact will either influence or determine our reaction. The margin of freedom in our response is a matter of percentages—for example, fifty-fifty, ninety-ten. In this book, we are focusing on triggers in the context of relationships, so catalyzing triggers are our topic, not causal ones. We are focusing on how we have resources, so choice will be our topic, rather than instances of no choice.

The New Age, pop-psychology assertion that we are fully in charge of all our feelings is a dangerous illusion. It insists that we are, or can always be, in full control. That is not in keeping with the implacable given of life that we are not. For instance, someone receives shocking news of the sudden death of a close friend or relative. A sane sensitive person will react with shock and grief. Her body will experience an automatic change in heart rate, breathing, pulse, brain synapses. This is a normal and appropriate human response. It is not something we can avoid nor is it healthy to try to control it. Likewise, I am sure that if any of us were to die unexpectedly and suddenly, we would like to believe that our family and friends would feel what loving people feel: shock and grief, as final tributes from those who care about us.

It is up to us to explore the origin of our triggered reflexes and work on moving past them. We can learn how to do this. It will take seeing a trigger as a pointer to our work rather than seeing it as simply a justified reaction. *In this way, a trigger arouses our curiosity about ourselves rather than only a reaction to others.* We find out exactly where to focus our energy so we can liberate ourselves from being hijacked by others' behavior. In other words, we become independent adults.

Each person has some unique trigger points. Some triggers are universal—though individual reactions may be quite diverse. Some common triggers, hot buttons most us will recognize, include the following:

- We are with people who are expressing their feelings (and we are especially triggered when the feelings are directed at us).
- We experience a sudden loss.
- We receive bad news.
- A natural disaster occurs.
- Someone is acting aggressively or violently.
- A person, place, or thing reminds us of a past distress or trauma.
- Books, movies, or songs may evoke feelings, arouse a memory, give us an insight, motivate a change, or set a mood. Movies or songs from our past may trigger nostalgia.

- We experience stress that leads to an addictive reaction (in this example, the trigger is not a cause but can be a catalyst).

Here are nine categories of triggers that most of us can relate to, with specific examples of how they arise.

Feeling Self-Conscious

- We are being humiliated or judged as inadequate.
- We are alone or part of a minority in a group that is different from us in gender, race, sexual orientation, religion, political alignment, financial status.
- We feel shame when we compare where we are in life to how far others have progressed.
- We go on guard when references are made in a conversation to age, status, health, grooming, clothes, looks, accomplishments.
- We are called upon for public speaking.

Being Discounted

- Our adult children do not want to spend as much time with us as we want them to.
- Someone is sarcastic toward us.
- We are scapegoated, ridiculed, mocked, teased, or baited.
- We are patronized, put down, shown contempt.
- We are disrespected (which may feel especially triggering if abuse or aggression is happening too).
- We lose face or are belittled or shamed (which may feel especially triggering if it occurs in front of others whose opinion is important to us).
- We are snubbed or slighted.
- We are stood up or stranded, kept waiting for an inordinate amount of time, have an appointment canceled at the last minute.

- Someone is acting as if we were not there, as if our words, feelings, actions don't matter.
- Our experience is not believed.
- Our stating of a fact, supported by logic and evidence, is denied.

Feeling We Are Controlled

- We are being controlled or are around someone who is controlling.
- We are being told what our reality is; someone is imposing his or her reality on us.
- Someone is making decisions for us; we are being told what we feel, what to do, or how to think.

Being Taken Advantage Of

- We are robbed or lose money by being fooled, cheated, or conned.
- We are not paid for a service or paid back for a loan.
- We are not given what we believe is our due.
- We are given less than what others have been given.
- We are lied to, tricked, duped, deceived, or betrayed.
- We are misrepresented, misunderstood, suspected, discredited, falsely accused.

Feeling Vulnerable

- People are not supportive of or shame us for our feelings.
- We are about to take a test or receive the results of one.
- We feel we have no recourse when others are unfair toward us or when we are facing overwhelming problems.
- We are cut off in traffic.
- Our passenger is acting as a backseat driver.
- We have an accident or near accident.
- Someone repeats an annoying habit or something she or he already agreed not to do—knowing it bothers us.

- A sexual experience brings up disturbing feelings and thoughts that linger in a confusing way.

Relationship Experiences

- We displease someone and fear consequences.
- We feel engulfed or smothered by someone's over-attentiveness.
- A person who matters to us tells us he or she is moving away.
- The person we love does not show up for us or turns on us.
- People who matter to us show that they are not in our corner or they side with others against us.
- Someone is minimizing or discounting the impact of what we are feeling.
- Someone fails to attune to our feelings.
- We unexpectedly see someone we recently broke up with, see her or his ad on a dating site, hear how well she or he is doing.
- Suddenly and unexpectedly we see or meet up with our ex-spouse or someone with whom we have an unresolved conflict.
- We notice that a person we were once so close to now acts in an indifferent or disengaged way toward us.

Boundary Concerns

- Someone is coming at us while drunk or on drugs.
- Someone is hitting on us or acting in an inappropriate or sexist way.
- Our boundaries are being crossed either in major ways, such as overriding a decision of ours, or in minor ways, such as sticking a fork into our dish to taste our food at the kitchen table or at a restaurant.
- Someone is rushing us, not respecting our timing.
- We are being scrutinized, interrogated, or hit with a barrage of questions, especially just as we arrive at home or work.

- Someone is trying to sell us something or convince us of something in a pushy way.
- Someone is acting as if he or she has authority when he or she does not (e.g., an older sibling trying to control us).
- Someone in authority refuses to acknowledge our right to be heard.
- Our saying "No!" is not being respected.

Feeling Uncomfortable about What Is Happening

- A family member or partner does or says something in public that embarrasses us.
- We are about to meet a new person.
- We are about to have sex with someone for the first time.
- Someone is talking about politics or religion in a way that is distasteful to us or contrary to our views.
- Someone is showing bigotry or telling a joke that puts others down.
- We are discriminated against, persecuted, or excluded because of our race, religion, economic status, political persuasion, gender, sexual orientation, physical or mental disability.
- We hear the news and strongly oppose what politicians and governing bodies are up to.
- We see someone harming an animal.

Fearing What Might Happen

- We are questioned, accused, or threatened by an authority figure such as a boss, the IRS, the police.
- Someone is using loaded words, actions, or gestures that have a judgmental or threatening impact.
- Someone comes at us with a facial expression that represents rejection or judgment—for example, a frown of impatience, disgust, reprimand, rage.

- There is a tone in the voice of someone that seems threatening, dismissive, condescending, curt (which may feel especially triggering if it reminds us of a tone one of our parents used toward us).
- We are triggered by a superstition or magical thinking. For example, we may believe that punishment is coming our way because we have done wrong or that rewards are owed to us because we have been good.

Some people trigger us without having to do any of the actions on the list above. The person's presence, or even the thought of the person, triggers a reaction. We might also be triggered if any of the events on this list happen to someone we love.

Some triggers have a double wallop. For instance, using an example from the list above, we tell our daughter about the danger of a drug she is using, and she refuses to listen. This triggers us, and we react with frustration but with compassion too. We then show the evidence using scientific articles. She replies, "You can believe what you want to believe." We are then triggered a second time because we know she is saying that we have no facts only opinions. We react with more frustration—this time with the sense that we are being discounted and patronized. Notice, in this example, as in all triggering experiences, that the other person pulls the trigger but how we are hit is up to us.

We notice also that every trigger on the list is a *given* of life and relationship—all triggers are. The list shows the way life is sometimes and the way people are sometimes. Givens of life include loss, unfairness, painful experiences, failed plans. A given of human interactions is the possibility of disappointment, rejection, abandonment, betrayal. None of us is entitled to a life with no triggers. All of us are vulnerable to others and to events. At the same time, fortunately, all of us have the inner resources to say in response, "Yes, it is this way and what is going on with me?" With that attitude we explore ourselves deeply rather than blame others uselessly. The more we accept reality with an unconditional yes, the less are we apt to be triggered.

Each of us has his or her own roster of triggers. What triggers us may be water off a duck's back to our friend. We see her respond with assertiveness and confidence to a slight that would throw us for a loop. We admire her and wish we could be like that. Actually, however, it could be that slights are not on her trigger list so in fact it did not take much courage for her to respond. When her buttons are pressed, she may react without the confidence we observed in this instance. Some of what we call courage and hutzpah is really about not being triggered into inhibition.

Triggers lead to self-doubt. We believe we cannot manage our feelings and reactions. We do not trust our inner resources. Accessing these tools, however, fosters a restoration of safety and security. Likewise, safety and security in a relationship can take what is ordinarily triggering and make it no big deal. What might have pierced us before now bounces off us.

As we saw above, triggers arouse grief: We are sad about a loss. We are angry at the one who caused it. We are afraid we will not be able to handle the empty space it has left in our life. An immediately aggressive reaction can be an avoidance of those components of grief. We then subvert an inner resource, our instinctive ability to mourn. We reduce our capacity to handle loss, disappointment, betrayal, hurt. As we allow ourselves to experience our grief and accept it as part of life, we can discover pathways through it. This increases our self-trust; we feel assurance that we have healthy resources and can access them appropriately when needed. Sometimes our reaction to a trigger leads us to violate our own principles. For instance, we suspect our partner is being unfaithful. We react with fear, hurt, and indignation. We then trespass over boundaries we would ordinarily honor. We search his cell phone, texts, emails. We do drive-bys. The healthy alternative is to tell our partner of our feelings and misgivings. We confront the concerns together in dialogue or in therapy.

Some triggers—for instance, being ridiculed in the presence of others—may not be restimulations of a past trauma; that is, they may not be the result of post-traumatic stress. They may simply be appropriate responses to a truly disturbing situation. We might then collapse in shame, become enraged, or retaliate. The healthy response, the response that can become a practice, is a mindful "Ouch!" without judgment or vindictiveness. By simply saying "Ouch!" we assertively, not aggressively, set our boundaries and seek dialogue. If there is no room for reasonable discourse our only healthy response is leaving the premises. A limbic atmosphere drowns out prefrontal dialogue!

REAL AND IMAGINED TRIGGERS

When we know we are triggered by something, unique to us or universal, we are on the lookout for it. This high-alert style may lead to our imagining what is not really there. For instance, we might judge others unfairly because we are basing our attitude or behavior on a faulty suspicion. Here is an example: Pascal comes from a family in which people did not have his back. His parents did not stand up for him, nor did they step in to protect him when needed. This led Pascal to be overly sensitive about whether his friends and partner could be trusted to back him up. On one occasion he imagined that they did not come through for him when they actually did. At a party, a coworker, Cole, was saying that Pascal had more talent than fit the job he was in. Cole was encouraging Pascal to look for work that would take advantage of his full range of creativity. Pascal's friends and his wife, India, heartily agreed. But Pascal felt Cole's comment as a put-down. He felt hurt that India and his friends did not speak up for him but agreed with Cole. At home, he projected blame onto India.

Often, blame in a relationship is based on misunderstanding or imagining a trigger that was never really pulled. In addition, blame is often a cover-up for grief. And grief is what Pascal was actually feeling. When India explained, Pascal realized he had it wrong. He then found comfort or relief, but that does not help him identify and work with the deeper patterns behind his trigger reactivity—only salve it. Pascal still needs help finding the useful path from painful trigger to personal work.

Some triggers are based on reality; some are based entirely on illusion. For instance, fear creates a distorted version of reality, something like the way the world looks to a colorblind person. We might react with a paranoid fantasy or belief to something that is not really a danger. We are triggered by something that is not happening—a situation like the one we saw in the example of Pascal and Cole.

Here is a personal example of how fear triggers and misleads. Once I was looking out my window into the backyard of my house in Duxbury, Massachusetts. I saw my cat, Keif, in distress mode, strongly arching her back and fiercely hissing. I saw no danger and wondered what she was reacting to. When I looked out another window, I realized what all the fuss was about. A gentle-looking cocker spaniel puppy had wandered into the yard. Not only did the puppy pose no threat; he also *didn't even see* Keif. So all the cat's gyrations and adrenaline reactions were in vain. Keif was triggered into fear mode when there was nothing fearsome happening. I remember thinking that the whole scene was a metaphor for some of my own fear reactions. My story shows that we, like the scared cat, can misread some triggers. Could it be that all our triggers are cocker spaniel puppies? Could it be that we are like Keif, afraid of what isn't harmful (and per-haps the thing she was afraid of would have only wanted to play)? Likewise, we too might feel fear at times even from a position of safety—normal for a cat and for us.

We are also triggered by an illusion when the meaning or level of seriousness we imagine does not match reality. Since we are caught in our own projections this mismeasurement will be well-nigh impossible to pick up on. Here is one example: Jamie tells her friend Casey that she is moving away by the end of the year.

Jamie's words are a trigger; Casey immediately has a sinking feeling in her stomach. Jamie's message is simply that she is leaving town; her decision was not meant to be an abandonment of Casey. Yet Casey feels it that way because her emotions do not distinguish between absence and abandonment. Any leaving is taken as abandonment, which exaggerates and mistakes its meaning. (A fear of abandonment doubles the impact of a trigger.) Casey will benefit from her reaction when she sees that grief is appropriate but feeling abandoned is a pointer to where her work is. This example brings to mind the psychologist Erik Erikson's 1950 book *Childhood and Society*: "Why do we think the face has turned away which only looked elsewhere?"

In a second example, the illusory interpretation of an experience is more subtle. Rocco is single though he wants to have a partner. He is trying to sublet his apartment for six months while he works in another city. Prospective renters come to view his place, but they choose other apartments. He is triggered into worry or panic. He realizes that he is to leave soon and thinks, "I still have no one." That phrasing can be a clue to Rocco that somehow he is mixing up a business transaction with relationship concerns. He is feeling rejected by the viewers who did not choose *him*, when actually they only did not choose the apartment. Rocco can work on how his sense of isolation or unworthiness has contaminated what has to be seen as a straightforward business enterprise.

We notice in both examples that we are triggered when we have not separated what is informational from what is personal. Likewise, in both examples, grief is appropriate, and the triggers help us look at our personal work. When a trigger accomplishes that nudge toward self-reflection, it is a true boon.

Casey and Rocco might tell their friends about how they were triggered. Their friends may rush to explain: "Oh, it wasn't meant that way." But that statement is addressed to the part of the brain based on reason, the prefrontal cortex. The trigger reaction is happening in the limbic system of the brain. So rational explanations do not work. The friends are speaking in cerebral to someone who now can only speak limbic. That part of us does not listen to reason, cannot listen to it. The work for Casey and Rocco will require a deep look into the primitive origins of their reactions and a reach into the appropriate feelings they have been avoiding.

As a final observation about our exposure to triggers, we could recall Aristotle's comment that we feel pity and fear when we are spectators at a stage tragedy. We are indeed triggered while watching plays or films. We notice ourselves reacting as if the events on stage were happening to us. We amp up or tear up based on what we see on the screen, but the story is actually our own. The drama has moved into us, unfolding robustly in the theater of our own wounded hearts.

Yet, we can react with feelings and then not have to engage in follow-up behaviors. At a horror movie, we feel fear, but we stay seated and we get over it when the next scene opens. Tears flow when the characters of a film endure misfortunes, but we don't collapse in despair. We become angry as we see them enduring injustice, but we don't protest or retaliate. This reminds us that we do have it in us to react to a trigger without having to act on it.

> The blood and baseness of our natures would conduct us
> to most preposterous conclusions: but we have
> reason to cool our raging motions.
>
> —Shakespeare, *Othello*

WHEN THE TRIGGER IS INSIDE US

A trigger can rouse us from the outside, what people do or how events provoke us. But sometimes the trigger is not in the room. It is internally aroused: We recall an event that was traumatic. We imagine what might happen in the near or distant future. We have a sense of guilt or shame and feel a fear of impending doom or punishment. We realize we hurt the feelings of a friend and we are triggered into the fear of losing her friendship. All of this might be illusory of course. We would have to check with our friend to find out if what she is feeling matches what we are believing.

Here is an example that shows how an internal trigger can connect to our childhood. Let's say that our boundaries were continually crossed in early life, including by having been abused. This leads to shortening of the spectrum between being *asked* to fulfill a person's need and feeling it as a *demand*. Without that background, the spectrum is wide; we easily see the difference. A friend asks for a favor, some form of support. We might hear her asking as demanding because of our habit of seeing these two as synonymous. Our wick is short so we easily become angry—and can't trust that our anger is justified. Instead, we can ask her directly if she is asking or demanding. If she is only asking, we can confess humbly, "I get these mixed up sometimes so I need others' help in discerning."

Here is one more example of the spectrum experience. We were not given healthy attention in childhood, only scrutiny—not watched over but patrolled. We did not feel supported but rather inspected, especially to find out if were staying on the straight and narrow. Later in life we might fear attention, no matter how sincerely it is given to us. Our spectrum of attention, from healthy caring concern to unhealthy scrutinizing, has been cut short. We are able to feel only the negative end of it, the *familiar* end. Now all forms of close attention are triggering. We feel threatened and we react with the same fears we felt in childhood.

This leads us to the following question: *Who* is triggered? It is not the woman who has become a brain surgeon and runs her department at the hospital. It is the little girl still inside her who was told over and over again how inadequate she was and would surely remain. It is not the man who has become a Buddhist monk and is trusted by his sangha to oversee many important tasks skillfully. It is the little boy who was controlled in his every move and trained not to trust himself. The little one inside us had her or his amygdala trained into fear, shame, and a sense of inadequacy before we had boundaries to fend them off. That child within is the one who is triggered. The big adult in the world is still often at the mercy of those internal conditionings no matter what her or his accomplishments, intelligence, or even self-confidence.

We might trigger ourselves in some of the following ways:

- Feelings arise in us, especially when they do so suddenly, surprisingly, or beyond our control.
- We have a gut feeling, premonition, suspicion, or intuition.
- We keep doing what we don't like ourselves for doing—for example, fishing for compliments, whining, manipulating, being too passive, getting caught in arguments with people who are closed to new knowledge.
- We can be triggered by our own sense of obligation. This can lead us to choices that do not reflect our own deepest needs, values, and wishes.
- We feel ashamed because we have disappointed someone, especially if it happened because we did not keep our word.
- An inner critic can trigger us into self-doubt or self-blame.
- A memory of a traumatic event, a mistake we made, something we did that we are not proud of sits in us as regret and that may trigger us to blame ourselves or, when appropriate, to make amends.
- A memory of a happy event or word of wisdom comforts us in times of difficulty or pain.
- If we did not let go of our caretaking style toward our adult children when the time for it came, we might now be triggered unduly by their independence from us or by their personal issues.
- Fears and phobias can be triggers into actions or rituals that we believe are useful when they may not be.

- A dream can trigger us both during the dream and when we awaken.
- Any one of our senses can trigger us. Our olfactory sense is particularly powerful and has a long-lasting memory. We can be easily triggered when we smell something that has an association with a past experience—for example, particular foods, perfume scents, flowers, human or household aromas, unpleasant odors.

Some triggers arise from our unconscious. They may take a while for us to catch onto consciously. They are based mostly on transference. This means unconsciously transferring onto a person in the present the feelings, expectations, or beliefs about a person from our past. Someone comes along who has the qualities, and sometime the looks, of the parent with whom we still have unfinished business. This time the trigger does not lead to a burst of anger or a withering in sadness or fear. It is much more subtle. We try to get that triggering person to come through for us, to relate to us, to show love for us as we wanted one of our parents to have done. If he or she is withholding or distancing, we are triggered and then might react even more impetuously in our demand on him or her. We use every crafty trick we know, every subterfuge we can pull off, to commandeer him or her to fulfill our need. Here is the contradiction, however. At the same time, we subtly *train* the other person to be more and more like our parent, which could mean his being more withholding. We train him to spurn us. We stay while he is stingy so we can see Dad's stinginess again. We may then reduce the size of our requests, finally begging for just a crumb of connection. Then, by the grace of a sudden enlightening moment, we realize how that person is indeed just like Dad and we understand what all the fuss we have been making is really about. Awareness releases us from the transference of the past onto the present. We see how today's trigger hearkens from the past. We see how our past has strong-armed its way into our relationship in the present and how we became triggered and hooked.

A major internal trigger reaction is grief, expressed or unexpressed. This trigger is well illustrated in the following scene from the TV program *M*A*S*H*: the medical unit's commanding officer, Colonel Sherman Potter, is aware that his soldier-patient has awkwardly attempted several times to commit suicide. One day, the colonel finds the soldier in the empty operating room fumbling with the anesthesia machine. He is trying yet again to kill himself. The colonel is triggered into anger and seizes the hose and mask from the soldier's hand. He then turns on the machine properly, pushes the mask onto the private's face, and says, "You've screwed up over and over so now I'll show you how to do this right. You want to die? OK, let's do it!" The soldier is triggered into shock and fear. He pushes the mask away shouting, "Are you crazy? Get away from me!" But the colonel keeps at it (though never intending to harm him). Suddenly, the young man bursts into tears and, burying his face in the older man's chest, he cries like a baby. At this, the colonel tenderly embraces him and quietly says, "Good, the part of you that wants to live is stronger than the part that wants to die." Here the poignant scene comes to an end. When I watched this episode, I realized something much more profound going on. I saw a connection between suicide and unresolved grief. *A person is more likely to contemplate suicide when he can't start grieving or can't end it.*

We bottle up our grief at times—that is, can't start feeling it. We perseverate in grief at other times—that is, can't stop feeling it. We repress it in a depressed state. We are possessed by it in a manic state. The soldier in the *M*A*S*H* episode finally allowed his grief to emerge fully. This freed him, probably for the rest of his life, from the need to destroy himself. The triggers of repressed or frustrated grief were no longer pointed at him. Instead, he was positively triggered into resolution.

We cannot overlook one other detail in the scene: the grief

happened in the arms of someone who cared. It is the combination of letting go into our grief *while we are held safely* that graces us with the full antidote to despair. What a paradox indeed: grief is our threshold into hope.

> Only if someone has her arms around the infant . . . can the I AM moment be endured, or rather, risked.
>
> —D. W. Winnicott, *Deprivation and Delinquency*

INNER DEMONS

> Some Buddhist masters wake themselves up with a practice in which they invite all the demons of chaos and disaster to visit them. My little self says, "I am not at that point," but a braver, more expansive self answers, "Maybe that is what I have already done."
>
> —Stephen T. Butterfield, *The Double Mirror: A Skeptical Journey into Buddhist Tantra*

An "inner demon" is a metaphor for an irreconcilable, disturbing, and relentless inner conflict. This is another example of an internally aroused trigger. An inner demon has its origin in the past. It can take many forms—for example, feeling haunted by regret, shame, nagging guilt, some terrifying past experience that obsesses us. Likewise, when we repress our traumas they turn into buried ghosts. These become inner demons because the cemetery is inside us.

An inner demon brings a gnawing sense of inner collapse, a chaos ever approaching, always clutching us. This condition feels like a war within us from which no truce or treaty is possible. An inner demon is a torturer that triggers both anxiety and a sense of powerlessness. It is ego dystonic—that is, we cannot integrate it into our sense of normality. It feels alien to us, like a sinister demon possessing us.

Inner demons can't be fully named. We are conscious of their presence, but we find it hard to describe what they consist of or what they want of us. An inner demon is ultimately an ineffable anguish. Since healing takes telling of our pain, inner demons are tough to banish.

Actually, inner demons are thought forms and paradigms our ego bought into and now plague us with. Inner demons can lead a person to addiction or other forms of escape, including suicide. An inner demon cancels our ability to protect ourselves with self-deception. We have to face it, no escape. Likewise, we may feel the demon knows us better than we know ourselves. But, he knows us in an unsupportive way—the worst way to be known.

However, inner demons are not alien—or threatening—to the higher self, our larger life beyond ego. Our wholeness can accommodate what our conscious ego cannot. We activate this aspect of ourselves by feeling grief about whatever trauma was inflicted on us. If the demon is a regret about something reprehensible, we allow ourselves, in the present, to feel contrition for what we did. We ask for forgiveness for the past. We make amends. We commit ourselves to changing our behavior for the future.

We love ourselves when we accept our own demons as legitimate players in our life drama. Then even our instability and sense of incompleteness can be welcomed. In the Buddhist tradition, the great teacher Milarepa tried at first to expel the demons from his home but finally conversed with them, and they were transformed into allies. Our inner demons can be transformed that way too.

Some of our demons are based on shame. We can distinguish shame from guilt. We often confuse these two experiences. They are important in our understanding of triggers because, as we shall see below, each leads to a different reaction. Likewise, each has its own unique protocol for healing. Here are the differences:

GUILT	SHAME
Is about action or inaction, what we have done or left undone	Is about who we are
Says, "I did what is wrong or bad."	Says, "I am wrong or bad."
Includes the primitive belief that we deserve to be punished	Includes a belief that we are unlovable, worthless, to be spurned
Is a judgment or verdict	Is a feeling
Can be a healthy response to our doing what is unethical	Goes back to early life when we were hurt and shamed without it being based on actual wrongdoing
Usually is about something we are aware of; we know what we did wrong	Can't be fully named; we don't quite know what is wrong with us
Has external effects	Is within us
Has to do with what we have done to others (guilt is about transactions with others)	Has to do with how we come across to others (shame is about our sense of ourselves)
Can include either hiding or admitting	Includes fear of being found out and feeling vulnerable to being harmed
Is culpability	Is self-negation
Includes awareness of how others are impacted by our behavior	Is an awareness of our own inadequacy, not necessarily based on others' reactions or opinions
Is triggered by our conscience	Can be triggered by criticism from others
Helps us be mindful of others and of the social contract; our sense of right and wrong keeps us on the upright path	Helps us avoid doing things that will turn us into an object of derision in society or make us lose our freedom; our fear of being shamed is a deterrent
Includes an underlying sense that there is a way of freeing ourselves such as confessing, being pardoned	Holds the sense that there is no way to let it go or be free of it
Can lead to being contrite and to making amends	Holds the pain inside and may project it onto others to reduce one's own shame
Leads to self-forgiveness once we have made our amends	Cannot let us forgive ourselves

Opens into a path to redemption	Finds no release from regret
Can lead to concern for others' feelings and rights	Can lead to depression or aggression
Can show caring for others	Can become hatred of ourselves or others
Can be completely removed by amends and self-forgiveness	Remains a wound until we grow in self-esteem and self-compassion
I was guilty of being mean toward others.	*I am ashamed that I am the kind of person who would be mean.*

A final word about guilt: Guilt inputted into us in early life from family or religion is a common internalized trigger. When the guilt is appropriate, we welcome information and recommendations that show us how to honor the social contract. When the guilt is inappropriate, we recognize that and learn to let it go. As full-fledged adults we realize that the purveyors of guilt about what was not really reprehensible—for example, self-pleasuring—were not ultimately concerned with our breaking a commandment. Their purpose was to gain and maintain control over us, especially over our bodies, genitals in particular. What is called "sin" in this instance is really about daring to defy authority by affirming our own power over our bodies. It seems that we were guilt-tripped into believing it was wrong to experience pleasure. We were warned that our sexual instinct was dangerous, could get us into trouble, including a place in hell. Adults see now what the threats were really about. We were being guilt-tripped about having personal power. We were not being taught what we really needed to know: how to use our power—or bodies—intelligently.

We see harmful teachings like these now without resentment toward those who inflicted them on us. We feel compassion for ourselves and for those who were afraid of losing their power over us. And we no longer hand it over to them, either. Instead, we form our own conscience with wisdom and with respect for ourselves and others. We give ourselves another chance at having and enjoying personal power. Then if we are still triggered internally by old inappropriate injunctions, we let ourselves feel the danger of offending (some unseen force) and do it anyway.

> Hell itself will pass away,
> And leave her dolorous mansions to the peering day.
>
> —John Milton, "On the Morning of Christ's Nativity"

WHAT MAKES TRIGGERS SO DISTURBING

Trigger reactions involve projection. We see ourselves in others but think it is entirely about them, not about us. In projection we are looking into a mirror of ourselves. It helps to use the analogy of viewing a movie. We feel attracted to or repelled by one of the actors. But the actor is not there! We are gazing at a picture of our own attractions or repulsions. We are doing the same thing the projectionist is doing, projecting. The difference is that he is doing it without being triggered by what he sees.

Most of the time a trigger hinges on what we imagine or believe. We imagine that what is happening is serious, threatening, sometimes even having life-or-death importance or consequence. For instance, if our ego has become indignant, we might believe the other person does not respect us as he should. Our belief can be, and often is, illusory. An experience can be carried over from the past and projected onto someone in the present. An example is fear of arousing a man's anger. When Dad started to become angry, a beating followed. Now we fear others' anger because our body fears a repetition of that original sequence. In other words, we predict an outcome based on past experience, not always an accurate forecaster. (Anger may indeed lead to violence in our present life, but that would be a coincidence not a given.)

Serious triggers hearken back to early trauma. Since triggers happen in the primitive brain, a recollection of a past moment seems totally real in the present. This is how they retraumatize us. When the original painful event occurred, we were unable to express our indignation. It was unsafe to show our feelings. We dissociated ourselves from them. Our reaction to a trigger in the present finally *enacts* our original but stifled scream of fear or anger. *A trigger gives us a chance to experience fully in the here and now what was interrupted in the past.* This is how the trigger experience can help us. The psyche, always on the look-out for an opportunity to heal and integrate, catches onto a trigger so that our original incomplete experience can be finished at last. D. W. Winnicott in "Fear of Breakdown" assessed it this way: "The original experience of primitive agony cannot get into the past tense unless the ego can first gather it into its own present time experience."

It is hard for any of us to see that the bigness, the wallop, of a trigger, does not indicate a comparable level of seriousness or importance. The wallop has gained its heft from past events. In addition, every time we give in to a trigger we reinforce and magnify its importance as well as the level of terror or rage it evokes.

At the psychological level, a trigger can ransack our sense of safety and security. It can feel like a death threat from which there is no escape. The stress increases when we can't find a way to fix the problem—that is, can't self-regulate. We feel a sense of powerlessness, even a sense that our world is falling apart, that we are falling apart. We lose our trust in ourselves. We find ourselves in a chaotic world of disorganized attachments to ourselves and others. This all happens because we are being forced to look at a trauma we are not yet prepared to face. We have been thrown into the deep end of the pool before we had learned to swim.

Dan Siegel, in his work on trauma therapy, coined the phrase "window of tolerance." This refers to trauma-managing, self-regulating, and self-soothing techniques that enable us to go through a threatening experience safely. A trigger closes, or at least narrows, our window of what we can tolerate. This happens because our prefrontal cortex has become temporarily disabled and its rational powers are not fully accessible. Its executive function is bypassed. Instead, the amygdala and limbic system in general take over. We therefore feel an emotional impact without access to all the subtleties of rational thought. When we go to our inner resources of self-adjustment and self-management our wise brain comes back into focus. Then our responses to the triggering event can become appropriate. Our window of tolerance has been reopened. We have space in which to hold an experience, contain it safely, and move through it securely and bodily too. The narrow window has widened.

Our reaction to a trigger is somatic, bigger than any thought. We feel it in our body—for instance in our breath, stomach, neck, jaw, and so forth. It happens internally, with heart rate, with brain synapses. Trigger points are indeed deeply embedded in our bodies: "The ego is first and foremost a bodily ego," Sigmund Freud wrote in *The Ego and the Id*. Some examples of a bodily triggered reaction are a stab of pain, losing one's temper, blushing, feeling nausea, feeling anxiety or panic, being stricken with grief. More serious reactions—for instance shock, stroke, heart attack—require a medical intervention.

We might be especially vulnerable to being triggered when we are already in distress: We are cranky, overtired, physically uncomfortable, irritable, frustrated, upset from a recent disturbing experience elsewhere. Our excessive reaction can lead us to make hasty or undiscerning decisions. We can lose our discriminating powers and act impulsively. Then, we may do or say something we will later regret. We may hurt someone's feelings. We may hurt ourselves.

The impact of triggering events is especially strong when we have not had enough sleep. The neuroscientist Matthew Walker, in his 2017 book *Why We Sleep*, writes, "Without sleep, our brain reverts to a primitive pattern of uncontrolled reactivity. We produce unmetered, inappropriate emotional reactions, and are unable to place events into a broader or considered context. . . . We cannot rein in our atavistic impulses—too much emotional gas pedal (amygdala) and not enough regulatory brake (prefrontal cortex)." Likewise, an excess of norepinephrine prevents REM sleep—that is, necessary deep sleep. In healthy sleeping, during the periods of REM sleep, our stress hormone, norepinephrine, becomes inactive. This prevents us from waking up during a stressful dream.

Triggers can be disturbing for another reason: In addition to personal triggers there are also collective ones. For instance, we might feel foreboding anxiety or indignant rage while visiting a historic site where terrible deeds were perpetrated. The archetypal energies linger there for years and, without an inner shield, we are in the line of fire. Our triggered reaction can even last a long time after our visit. We are carrying the grief of the original tragedy still sparking with haunted hurt.

Some triggers work positively to marshal an energy in us that may have lain dormant up until now. For instance, we are in a situation in which someone is being victimized. Suddenly, we access the courage to step in and protect him. The human hero energy has been galvanized.

As a practice we might ask this question when we are triggered: What part of me is ready to be activated by this? This expands our self-esteem because we notice our wealth of inner resources.

The best news, as we have been seeing, is that every trigger shows us what our psychological or spiritual work is. In this sense, every trigger is an example of synchronicity, the meaningful coincidence between the trigger and our finding out what we have to address, process, and resolve—all in accord with the appropriate timing and our own readiness, of course. How do we address, process, and resolve a problem or issue?

- To address is to look at it what is going on without attempting to avoid, deny, or escape it. We admit what we are up to. We name our feeling, concern, trigger, reaction, addiction, longing. Neither Winken nor Blinken nor Nod is onboard.

- To process is to experience and express any feelings we have about the problem. This includes seeing how they may hearken back to our childhood. We look at our projections, transferences, and defenses. We look into our traumas to whatever extent we are ready to do so. We explore the origins of our triggers and reactions. We do this with the diligence of fearless spelunkers, no corner unexplored however dark.
- To resolve a personal issue is to make a change for the better. We work on ways not to react inappropriately to triggers but to respond effectively to whatever happens. To resolve an issue in a relationship is to hear one another and open to one another's feelings. We make an agreement that leads to more mutually acceptable interactions in the future. We let go of any need to resent, retaliate, or hold a grudge. We may then notice ourselves entering a serene enlightened space.

As a final review, here is an at-a-glance picture of our topic so far:

Trigger
The stimulus takes the form of a word, gesture, experience, action, or event that makes us feel unsafe and insecure.

Impact and Belief
We experience an emotional impact based on a belief, usually exaggerated, sometimes mistaken altogether, that the stimulus is important, crucial, imperative to act on.

Reaction
Our reaction can be an *emotion* such as sadness, anger, fear, shame, regret. It can also lead to a *behavior* such as raging, attacking, retaliating, placating, kowtowing, yielding, breaking into tears, falling apart, fleeing, fighting, freezing.

The more important a person is in our lives the stronger is the impact of a trigger from her and the longer-lasting our reaction. We are healthy people when we let people matter, especially those who are close to us. But sometimes we bring someone too far into ourselves, we overvalue their opinion, we dissolve appropriate borders between us and them. Then we are vulnerable to being overly triggered by what they say or do. Our human challenge with all our fellow humans is to seek a balance between caring and boundaries.

Resources

We can marshal our internal and external resources to help us work effectively with our trigger reactions. The following chapters focus on how we can steadily build these resources.

TWO
TRAUMAS AND RESOURCES

We are turtles, not birds. We take our childhood home with us
wherever we go. We cannot fly away from it.

Now we can look more deeply at points we addressed earlier in
this book. We see them in the context of trauma.

A trigger takes us by storm when it reinstates painful experiences from early life. Our more hard-hitting trigger points may
have been implanted by abuse or trauma that happened in the past
or in our adult life and are now archived deep within our somatic
memory. Such post-traumatic stress is difficult to unseat because
a trigger restimulates the original pain. The good news is that our
pain is coming from a helpful scalpel not a mugger's switchblade.
It is a nudge, a prompt to approach our healing work.

CHILDHOOD WOUNDS AND NEUROSCIENCE

"Trauma" is the Greek word for wound. A trauma is a shocking,
injuring event. It evokes severe distress that we are powerless to
avoid. We become immobilized or we react with a sudden feeling
or un-thought-out choice. Trauma is really more about our reaction than about the causal event. The reaction is our sense of not
being in control, helpless, powerless: "I can't do anything about
this. I am trapped. There is no escape or exit."

In the original trauma experience we probably dissociated
ourselves from what was happening. This makes the memory of

it difficult to retrieve. It also explains why trauma takes so much time to absorb and resolve. It can take years to see what our original trauma was, then take more time to feel the feelings we have kept repressed, and more time again to resolve what is still unfinished. None of this can happen until our inner clock tells us we are ready to address our pain, a readiness that may take years to kick in. Trauma therapy thus involves titrating, letting the impact in little by little. As Shakespeare's character Iago asked in *Othello*: "What wound did ever heal but by degrees?"

A trigger, however, disregards our timing and hurls us into our trauma suddenly, before we are ready. This is why it retraumatizes us. A trigger is a bull in a china shop, canceling our carefully built-up—and often necessary—mechanisms of avoidance or titration. Now we understand why we have a regressive reaction, why we feel such childlike powerlessness. A trigger-trauma is an example of something happening to us that is too big for the resources we have gathered so far. For healing to happen a trauma has to feel like a gentle Bambi energy or memory in us rather than Godzilla stomping on us.

Since trauma is recorded somatically, our bodies know better than our minds what is really happening when we are triggered. For instance, we might become numb in reaction to an attack. We later think we were cowardly. Actually, our reaction was an adaptive measure to a cue too subtle for the brain but easily grasped by our body. The body's reaction takes precedence over strategizing by the brain. It may not read the events correctly since it assesses a trigger as dangerous on the basis of memory rather than on updated information. But we still don't need to blame ourselves. We understand that the body has only our survival in mind. Next time we are triggered we can find a way to honor our autonomic reaction and still take a stand.

Thus, triggers, based on trauma or on any distressing experiences, show us where the past invades the present. We can work with a trigger and thereby look directly into the hidden world of who we are, how we came to be the way we are now, how to heal ourselves, how to enter the present without the past standing in the way. Then trigger reactions turn our wounds into entryways. We are thankful we can learn from our sufferings, even find consolation through what originally hurt us. We hear in Psalm 23: "Thy *rod* and thy staff, they *comfort* me."

Along these lines, we remind ourselves of the term "post-traumatic growth." This is a concept from the psychologists Richard Tedeschi and Lawrence Calhoun from the University of North Carolina in their 2013 book *Post-Traumatic Growth in Clinical Practice*. We can focus on our resilience, not only our trauma—on our ability to gain from our experience and thereby evolve beyond where we were in our pain. The pain following trauma does not have to knock us out; it can awaken our inner resources. A wise therapist may help us here.

HEALTHY WAYS TO CONNECT OUR THEN AND NOW
Acknowledge Influences from Childhood

When childhood issues arise, a trigger that seems like a transaction might actually be a recollection:

Transaction: "You triggered me when you criticized me."

Recollection: "I am triggered by criticism into a feeling of shame about my inadequacy. This reaction points me to my own work since it reminds me of how Mom came at me in childhood." We might then say to ourselves or to the other person: "But wait! You are only the most recent version of a long series of unfinished experiences of criticism going all the way back to my earliest transactions with women. Thank you for showing me what I need to revisit and integrate. I appreciate an opportunity like this. Please don't make it easy on me by softening your comments. The criticisms are helping me lessen the impact they have on me. Then we will surely find more effective ways to communicate. I don't want to become stoical or indifferent to your comments. Ultimately, my goal in all this is to care more and be triggered less.

That makes my work more than just about childhood; it is about fostering intimacy."

When we are triggered, we can't reach common ground. We might wonder if getting triggered is a sly way our scared ego has of making ourselves safe from closeness? We will revisit this in a later chapter.

The Five As

The first way, or practice, is to explore the five As, our earliest needs: attention, acceptance, appreciation, affection, allowing. We look at how these needs were or were not fulfilled in our childhood. We respond in detail, with at least one example, to each of the following elements of the five As in a journal. We distinguish which parent fulfilled the needs, if only one of them did. Remember that no one will give a perfect score to his or her parents.

The five As outlined below are the elements of an *ideal* holding environment, the qualities of secure attachment. This is not meant to describe the usual experience of a childhood. Fortunately, as children we can experience safety and security and have our needs satisfied with "good enough" parenting. We do not need perfection, nor is it possible.

Yet, when there were major deficiencies in early life we find grist for the mill of our personal work of grief and then self-parenting. As part of this work we let go of blame or resentment toward our parents for their inadequacies.

If you are a parent, you may want to use the listings below to look into your own parenting style. Share this practice with your children if they are old enough to understand it. Ask them for an honest take on your parenting of them and open a dialogue about it.

Finally, the five As also describe what we need from our adult partners. You can, therefore, adapt the following points to your relationship needs and longings: you to your partner, your partner to you. Again, we healthy adults are satisfied with good-enough, not perfect. In the "True Companions" section in chapter 7 there is more help with this topic.

Here are some ways our parents might have fulfilled our needs for the five *A*s in childhood. Each is stated as an ideal. All are to be understood as including healthy limit-setting:

Attention

You felt that your parents, or at least one of them, directed an engaged focus on you.

You felt they were paying mindful attention to you with no judgment or reproach of you.

They looked not at you but into you to know your feelings and needs.

They asked you what you felt and needed without trying to convince you otherwise.

They attuned to your feelings and needs in a mirroring way.

They checked in with you about your reactions to them and to family events.

You knew you would be heard, that your story and emotions were of genuine interest to them and would always have a welcoming response.

They loved knowing you.

Acceptance

You knew that whatever you were or would turn out to be was acceptable to them.

You knew they were not trying to make you into what they wanted you to be but instead were curious about what you yourself would grow into.

They showed you that your interests were totally acceptable to them.

They accepted your feelings, needs, lifestyle.

They accepted your sexual and gender orientation with no reprimand or suggestion you be otherwise than what you were.

All your feelings were OK with them, rather than some being judged as wrong—for example, "Boys don't cry."

You were not shamed.

You did not have to try to fit in to the family; you always knew you belonged—no matter how different you were.

Appreciation

You were valued by your parents for yourself, not for your accomplishments.

You did not feel that you were a burden or "another mouth to feed."

Your parents did not play favorites.

They appreciated your uniquely important place in their lives and in that of the whole family.

They acknowledged your gifts, gave you credit for them, did what they could to boost them.

Your parents backed you up if and when others turned against you.

They understood your joys and tears and held them in an equally warm embrace.

You knew you could always trust them.

Affection

Your parents hugged, held, and kissed you.

They showed their love in physical ways without being inappropriate.

You often heard them tell you that they loved you.

No one was embarrassed by eye contact or touch.

You felt that your experience was cradled with benevolent fondness ever-expanding.

You knew without a doubt that your parents' caring
connection to you would never end.
They welcomed affection from you in your way of showing it.
Their ways of showing love evolved in accord with your age
but never lessened in sincere tenderness.
You know they had wanted you even before you were born
and that they always will.
You felt you were irreplaceable.

Allowing

Your parents tried their best to know your deepest needs,
values, and wishes.
They were not insisting that these needs, values, and wishes
had to mirror their own.
They were not trying to control you, but they did set
reasonable limits to guide you.
You felt free to explore the world around you rather than
being held back or obliged to caretake them.
They loved having you find new ways of thinking and
imagining even when your ways did not match theirs.
You were approved of whether you were marginal or
mainstream in your lifestyle.
You could trust your parents to encourage you in your
personal journey and to support you in it.
They provided a safe home to be in or come back to while
launching you out of it when you were ready.
You knew they would help you fulfill your life goals by
contributing, in whatever way they could, to your finding
your unique path in the world.
They could let you go.

Can I now love others—and myself—in these same ways?

As a practice, whenever we happen to remember an instance
of our parents showing us one or more of the five *A*s, we can

say internally, "I appreciate how you loved me. May I show myself, you, and others that same love." In this statement we show appreciation for our parents *and* extend it into a loving-kindness practice toward ourselves and others. Whatever love we receive from anyone can encourage us to give it to everyone.

> How grateful I am for [my mother's] buoyant example, for the strong feeling of roots she gave me, for her conviction that, well-grounded, you can make the most of life, no matter what it brings.
>
> —Marion Rombauer Becker, *The Joy of Cooking*

Searching Questions

The second practice is to ask yourself the following twelve questions, ponder them, and write your responses in your journal. Exploring them in detail will help you realize how some of your childhood upbringing is still influencing your adult relationships. This is the same as asking how much of who you are in the world is the real you:

1. What is unresolved in my own life that I am imagining being in a relationship might fix?
2. How does my own story about my family of origin influence my sense of who I am now?
3. How does my experience with my own parents influence my way of being with others?
4. What attitudes from my family have remained in me and now influence my ability to accept others as they are?
5. How were these feelings expressed in my childhood: sadness, anger, fear, or joy?
6. How comfortable or uncomfortable am I with each of these four feelings in others?
7. How am I comfortable or uncomfortable with any of these feelings in myself?

8. How skillful am I at stating and maintaining personal boundaries?

9. How do my family biases get in the way of accepting those who differ from me politically or religiously?

10. What behavior can lead me to become so judgmental that I find it hard to feel or show compassion for another person's plight?

11. How skilled am I becoming in self-parenting or in parenting my own children?

12. How much and what of me reflects my own deepest needs, values, and wishes?

After I answered these questions, I asked myself what makes me happy about myself in these later years of my life. I answered this way: "I am happy that I have had my chance to be this person I am."

HOW MUCH OF ME IS ME?

A person wishes to be confirmed in his being by another person. . . . Secretly and bashfully, he watches for a Yes which allows him to be and which can come only from one human person to another. It is from one human being to another that the heavenly bread of self-being is passed.

—Martin Buber, "Distance and Relation"

Triggers point to unresolved conflicts. Resources help us hold our conflicts and heal them. How do triggers and resources relate to childhood issues? Here are some of the experiences in childhood that lead us to a healthy adulthood: Our feelings and personal qualities are honored, mirrored, attuned to. Our parents are admirable, and we idealize their greatness. We merge with it so that we too feel powerful. As we take over more and more of their functions, from tying our shoes to comforting ourselves in distress, we grow to be their peers. All this moves us from dependency to interdependence, from seeing ourselves as grandiose to having healthy self-esteem, from distrusting our feelings and intuitions to trusting ourselves more and more.

Our inner resources are not accessed in a vacuum. They come to us from the hands and hearts that love us. We touch into our inner resources most profoundly when we are fully ourselves. Since we all have parents and a history, we automatically carry traits and attitudes that have been inserted into us from them—some assets, some liabilities. No one is only an individual identity without past influences that have affected her personality. "Am I impersonating my mother when I judge others this way? Am I impersonating my father when I react this way?"

We are free from our parents' and others' influence when who they were to us is no longer inhibiting our choices, diminishing our self-esteem, ruling our adult relationships, invading our peace of mind, designing our behavior. When all these are free of any drag on them from parents or anyone else, we are released into being ourselves, our best resource. In that *freedom to be* we are less easily triggered by the past. We are so lucky when we have lost, one by one, all the mighty fortresses offered by churches, institutions, and parents because now we can be explorers of our own real world within.

Likewise, we know we have become full-on adults when the long-standing issue we have had with a parent is no longer something we have to work on *with* him or her. There is a time for family therapy. Hopefully, in that setting a parent hears us and, optimally, apologizes for any harshness inflicted on us in childhood. But with or without that helpful experience, as the years roll on, our resentment about how our parent treated us becomes our issue only. It is no longer a transaction requiring his or her participation or remorse. It is now a personal issue to be explored internally. We are adults when we have stopped blaming Mom or waiting for Dad to say the magic words that will "make it all better." We ourselves are now the only Ali Baba left standing at the cave of resources that can make us rich from here on in.

Maybe some tranquil day we might muse about our parents: "Nothing you have said or done or will say or do now takes away my peace of mind or lessens my self-esteem."

In the 1942 film comedy *I Married a Witch*, Jennifer is a witch and her alcoholic father is a warlock. He dislikes her choice of a husband and continually upbraids her. He wants to upset and end their union. Jennifer tricks her father into entering a bottle of alcohol. She then stoppers the bottle so he can no longer interfere with her or her relationship. But Jennifer places the bottle on the mantle in the living room of her marital home. Thus, her parent remains in the house but can no longer cause harm to her or her relationship. This is a metaphor for our relationship to our parents. We are never free of our connection to them, for good or ill. But when we are no longer under their influence or badgered by their opinion, we can have our own relationship in our own home. Their presence remains but it is safely bottled; it won't go away but neither can it cause harm.

At the same time, as adults we can see that our present problems cannot be blamed on how our parents acted, except in cases of severe trauma that still debilitates us in some way. We do not react to ourselves and others based on what our parents were like. Our trigger-reactions arise out of what we are still holding onto from what happened to us in their home. Thus, a way to be free of childhood influences is to separate the opinion of Mother about us from the reality of who we were and are. This is part of the work we do in therapy on childhood issues. We might explore such questions as these: "Was it safe to be me?" "Was I loved as myself or as the self they demanded I be?" "Did my parents patrol me or hold me?" "Did my parents acknowledge me for my accomplishments or for being me?" "Do I now see myself as my parents saw me or as I really am?"

We can use the metaphor of our past life being a school. Some of the childhood courses were these:

Who Are You?

How Relationships Work

Money

Sex

Food

The teachers had such authority and drilled us so often that the curriculum information was imprinted into every cell of our bodies. None of these five "courses" can ever be expected to be fully updated or resolved. But we can explore and gradually break most of the old ties. Here is an analogy: The times tables were drilled into our minds so that now it is impossible to hear "What is six times six?" and not think "thirty-six." Likewise, the attitudes we inherited from our parents govern how we see ourselves, our relationships, money, sex, and food. Both the information from grammar school regarding the three *R*s and the attitudes about the five topics from our unofficial "homeschooling" are deeply ingrained. We can't and don't want to change the grammar school information. But we *can* gradually change the homegrown attitudes. It is a slow process because the attitudes are automatic, mostly not in our conscious awareness. But it can be done, however tediously and awkwardly. Therapy and self-help techniques are our resources.

Most of us are not accustomed to being really free, not in childhood nor even now. Being in a family in which we are loved allows and encourages our freedom to be who we are. This allowing style of love is both conditional and unconditional. Our loving parents set limits on us—conditions—and we learned boundaries. They loved us unconditionally and we learned that we were worthy of love. Their constant "yes" to who we were led to self-esteem. Their occasional "no" to all we wanted to do fostered personal discipline.

We are also aware of roles in our family life: We might find ourselves playing the role of the caretaker or the victim or the rescuer. When we have an established role, we actually gain a sense of power. We are important now to the family; our place is secure. We noticed that being who we are did not succeed in making us valuable to other family members. Fidelity to our role becomes our way of being important: "I can't be loved here as I am but when I play the part they want me to play, I feel loved." Eventually we may realize that a role is a makeshift version of importance. Importance is a wannabe version of feeling loved. And both are dollar-store versions of authentic power.

As a humorous aside, we might hear ourselves say that our parents implanted a belief in us that we are unworthy. We declare that, as a result, we now believe we are indeed undeserving. But when it comes time to reward ourselves with a late-night treat, we have no problem convincing ourselves we "deserve it!" Perhaps this contradiction can now bring us to a shrug and a smile—two essential ingredients of contentment.

THREE

HOW TO HANDLE A TRIGGER

Between two and three million years ago our ancestors learned to make and use tools. Since then every generation has invented more and more sophisticated implements. Today, we own a collection of sophisticated tools to handle household or automotive needs. We also care for our tools, store them for future use, and add to our collection when necessary. Some of us have only a minimal collection; some of us have the full complement of instruments that outfit us for almost any hardware challenge that may arise. We are also able make tools in a pinch when ordinary tools can't do the job or are not available. We might have some tools we don't know how to use to their full capacity. All these options are a metaphor for our inner resources, the human toolbox. Thus, each of us stores useful inner tools, strategies to handle the challenges that come to us from people, events, and circumstances. We might have a minimal or a state-of-the-art collection. We sometimes have to invent our own tools in the face of crises that the self-help movement doesn't adequately address. We care for our toolbox by upgrading our knowledge and skill level through practice, as we are learning so far in this book. We have some inner resources we have not yet used to their full capacity.

We can learn how to make, use, upgrade, care for, and store the tools that can work for a lifetime. Without tools we are at the mercy of many triggers. With tools ready at hand we deal with what happens with grace and effectiveness. We can trust that we all have tools, inner resources. For instance, we have noticed that we have it in us to handle bad news. We know this because we hear or read of bad news daily and we are still able to get on with our day.

The hammer in my own toolbox belonged to my grandfather. This touches into the tool metaphor, also. Some of our inner resources are passed down to us from our forebears. Some families have qualities that survive the generations—for example, being unafraid to speak up in protest against injustice. A solidarity with all humanity is an example of a splendid spiritual asset. In other words, we ourselves feel the sting of injustice felt by an oppressed group. This is an example, by the way, of being triggered in a healthy way.

We know we were born with innate resources. We could cry out our needs without yet having the advantage of words. We could find the breasts that kept us alive without a map. Here is a simple way to remind ourselves that we had resources from the beginning of our lives: Close your eyes and picture yourself being carried across the room as an infant. Now picture yourself crawling across the room. Then picture yourself trying to walk across, falling, getting up again, and finally walking successfully. Open your eyes with the knowledge that you had and still have the inner resource of moving along on life's journey even though you occasionally fall.

We trust ourselves more and more when we notice that we can activate inner resources. We gain self-esteem when we notice that our inner resources help us handle our experience satisfactorily. As long as we avoid responding to our life events, we do not access our innate resources. We access them only when we fully enter our experience and take the clue it offers us on how to work through it. And there will always be a clue. For instance, loss evokes grief, injustice provokes anger, threat arouses caution.

In addition to innate resources, we have learned resources. These arise through trial and error, experience, and modeling from others. They can be psychological and spiritual: Our psychological—personal—resources are coping skills, abilities to handle life experiences without being destabilized by them. These are adaptive ways of regulating ourselves and managing our feelings, life skills that we continually have to replenish. Some examples are integrity, assertiveness, communication, know-how, forming a healthy ego, resilience, handling our own or others' feelings, and a variety of relationship skills.

We have inner spiritual resources too—capacities such as universal love, letting go of ego, a sense of service, compassion, and a treasury of core values to live by. As with all our innate resources it is up to us to translate them into practice.

Here is a surprising and encouraging realization: "Psychological" and "spiritual" are distinct but not oppositional. They are correlative aspects of the same reality of wholeness. For instance, integrity and universal love work together for our benefit, though the former is assigned to psychology and the latter to spirituality. Likewise, a psychological insight can lead to a spiritual practice. For instance, what triggers us into suffering can arouse our compassion for others who are triggered in the same way.

HANDY TOOLS

Some specific tools, both psychological and spiritual, help us respond rather than react to triggers:

- Naming is a primary way of dealing with any trigger. Making a list of our familiar, often-repeated triggers leads us to be on the lookout for them, to have a plan to deal with them: "This is one of my triggers so let me be careful not to overreact but instead to handle it this way . . ." We are catching the trigger red-handed and are ready to deal with it without being devastated by it. We can now immediately distinguish between what happened factually from what impacts us personally. In addition, the practice we have planned to handle a particular trigger can then come between stimulus and reaction. We make a conscious response rather than act on reflex. This escape from compulsion is our getaway to freedom. To find out Rumpelstiltskin's name is to be free of his threats. Keeping a journal of triggers and our (hopefully, changing) reactions is useful as we stay on this path toward freedom.

- We note our triggers in our journal along with our usual reactions to each of them. We dub each trigger entry a given of life, something that can happen to anyone: "I can expect that this might happen . . ." After each reaction entry we write, "I have many options in how I can respond." Now we see that we don't *have to* fall into a habitual reaction. That is a transition from compulsion to freedom. It is, by the way, the same transition we make to free ourselves from fear.

- We can become aware of the two reactions we might have to a trigger. The first is running away; the other is moving toward in a grasping or controlling way. We recall that these are also the very reactions that in Buddhism are said to lead to suffering: We run because we are possessed by fear or we cling because we are caught in craving. Yet both can light the way into dark and ancient caves that await us as we become ever-more-skillful spelunkers.

- Finding the source of a trigger—for example, a specific event, trauma, or transference—is central to freeing ourselves from it. In my own experience I notice that when I accurately locate where my trigger came from I reduce its wallop sometimes by as much at 70 percent! In fact, now I occasionally find what used to trigger me amusing.

- Working on the original trigger goes a long way to end its power over us. We take ownership of our triggers by engaging in the work, often lifelong, to resolve them. What remains alien, "all about them," keeps us stuck in separateness; what we acknowledge as our own we are able to heal and let go of.

- Triggers create hyper-arousal. Cortisol and adrenaline are coursing through us and affecting our brain negatively. In that stressed and destabilized state we feel safe only with the familiar; we are afraid to try new things. So we lose both ways. As we saw earlier, it is normal to feel fragile, disorganized, and disoriented when we are strongly triggered. It is true that we then seem to have no access to our inner resources—we can't self-regulate, we believe we are defective, we are left without a go-to. We can find inner resources nonetheless. We can use relaxation techniques—for instance, a series of deep breaths.

- When we are triggered by the inner critic we do not reply with an opposing opinion. That reaction will tie us into a web of back-and-forth with a voice trained much better than we in how to put us down. Instead, we use the inner critic's commentary about us as a call, a bell that reminds us to perform a spiritual practice, such as loving-kindness. For instance, the voice tells us we will "fail as we always have." We neither argue nor agree. We go directly to our affirmation: "I trust myself to do the best I can and to handle what happens." Now the voice of the inner critic is a skillful means to help us evolve.

- We can trust an inner healthy voice that advocates for us and is not critical of us. We are accessing not only the voice of sanity and reason but also the voice of encouragement that builds self-esteem. We can talk to ourselves like a kindly aunt or uncle. We distinguish what is happening from how we are feeling or believing things to be. We comfort ourselves and show understanding rather than rebuke ourselves for feeling so weakened by the reactions a trigger evinces.

- We apply our self-advocating voice as an override to obsessive thoughts, especially fear-triggering ones. When we hear ourselves saying, "The worst will happen," we interrupt—pave over it—with "I have it in me to handle whatever happens."

- Our self-advocacy includes giving ourselves the five As: We are attentive to what we are feeling. We accept it fully and fearlessly. We appreciate its life-lesson quality. We feel loving compassion for ourselves no matter how we are triggered or how we are reacting. We allow ourselves to take the next step on our journey rather than be stopped by the trigger.

- In mindfulness we attend to what happens or what we think or feel rather than become overwhelmed by it. In mindful moments, we don't identify with our reaction. We are *witnesses* of others, events, and ourselves. Our mindfulness extends both to triggers and to our reactions. We are mindful when we pay attention to and focus on the here and now without censorship, judgment, fear, reactiveness, attachment, or repulsion. Mindfulness helps us locate the pause between a trigger and a reaction. With this mindful style we are also less likely to react so excessively.

- Triggers evoke exaggerated or inappropriate emotional reactions. Our emotions are like muscles. They develop in healthy ways by being used appropriately. When we have hidden our anger most of our lives, for example, it becomes stunted. This is one reason why a reaction may come out as awkward and exaggerated when we are triggered. As we practice knowing and showing our emotions we will be less likely to react inappropriately to what triggers them.

- When we are triggered, we lose our objectivity and the wind may be knocked out of us. Thus, we can't easily be assertive and say "the right thing." We can reduce our reaction considerably when we take a breather. We let our ego calm down. Only when our ego is on hold can we respond to others with a nonjudgmental reporting of the impact of their behavior on us. Our assertion will then be much more rational. We access our inner resource of self-calming patience and we are not so strongly triggered next time. Hamlet's mother made this recommendation to him:

O gentle son,
Upon the heat and flame of thy distemper
Sprinkle cool patience.

- When someone triggers us by shaming, insulting, or hurting us, we can use the following technique (although it is difficult to remember to do this!): We simply repeat aloud to him very slowly the exact words that triggered us. We do this with a musing tone and with our eyes closed. Then we establish eye contact and keep looking directly at the person in silence as if awaiting his response. This is an example of how we create the pause that can prevent us from being bowled over so easily or feeling so victimized. In an aikido style, we are directing the energy back to its origin. This technique also gently confronts the other with his own words so he can feel how they landed on us.

- Family members are experts at triggering us. They know every one of our buttons and exactly how and when to push them. They keep their fingers on the nuclear reactors and it is no wonder that we are affected so strongly when we are with family members. Being on the lookout, fending off while remaining loving at all times, is our practice. Being present but only until the firing begins and then vacating the premises is how we protect our boundaries. We are, in effect, raising our hand with a signal of "No!" as a traffic cop does. The officer's purpose and ours are the same: not judgment or scolding but safety for all.

- Triggers thrive on our belief that we are alone in having them. They lose a major amount of their power when we realize that people we trust and admire are triggered in the same ways we are. Even enlightened people and saints can be triggered. Sharing with a trusted friend what our triggers are can lead to our being mirrored by him or her. That goes a long way to reducing the wallop of a trigger. All of us *feel* alone at times but we can trust that no one *is* alone in a world so interlaced as ours.

- As we saw above, to say that similar triggers happen to all of us is to acknowledge that they are givens of life. Therefore, our practice of accepting the things we cannot change—for instance, that people will say or do things that can arouse us—is a way of working with triggers. We don't allow abuse but do take it in stride that triggering experiences will happen. Our attitude of yes to that fact goes a long way toward reducing the power of triggers over us.

- We look for something humorous in our reaction to a trigger.

- It is human to take things personally when they are aimed at us that way. Our healthy practice is to feel our grief about how someone has hurt or offended us—and to say "Ouch!" Steeling ourselves against vulnerability does not help us since it is a way of avoiding appropriate grief.

- Therapy with someone who is trained in techniques to work with trauma, including somatic therapy and EMDR (eye movement desensitization and reprocessing), is also effective and often necessary.

It may be difficult to remember that we have these resources. This is because they reside in the part of our brain that is offline when a trigger assails us. We will need a daily visible reminder—for example, a note on the fridge saying, "When you are triggered, you have resources." We can then name a resource we have learned from this book. This suggestion works especially well when we are aware of our main triggers. Then, when they click in, we are more likely to go to the practices that help us deal with our triggers. As we saw above, triggers can change from being on-ramps into reactions to becoming trusty bridges into healing.

SHADOW, EGO, EARLY LIFE: WHAT'S REALLY GOING ON?

Some triggers target one or more of three specific areas inside us: our shadow side, our inflated ego, and our unfinished past. These areas can be the sources for trigger reactions. For each of them there are specific practices, in addition to the practices described above, that help us handle the associated trigger-reactions. In this section we will look at these three sources and find the resources to handle them.

Let's begin with a look at what is meant by each of the three:

Shadow: The negative "shadow" is a Jungian term referring to the unacceptable traits, desires, impulses, attitudes in our personality that have been repressed, disavowed, or denied. We do not want to admit we have what is called a "dark side." It remains unconscious. But when we see it in someone else, we react with criticism or anger. Actually, we are looking at another person as a mirror that forces us to see what we don't want to see in ourselves. Unfortunately, this projection is the equivalent of not being able to integrate our shadow side because then it seems alien, entirely outside us. When our reaction to how someone triggered us is such a projection we are looking at a shadow issue in ourselves. For instance, we do not see that we are controlling in our relationships. When someone else is openly controlling we are triggered and react. We fail to see that we are looking at a picture of our own controlling style. Both the trigger by someone and the reaction from us point to something that we have not yet admitted and integrated in ourselves.

Ego: Our ego can be healthy or at times dysfunctional. It is referred to as inflated when we become arrogant or think of ourselves as above others. We might strut and swagger, thinking we are too big to fail. When someone pulls us down a peg or two, therefore, it triggers a reaction of indignation in us. Behind that is fear that we are being found out to be less than we say we are, or less than we want to believe we are. We are panicked because we seem to be losing our entitlement to honor and recognition, losing our status as a big shot. Our reaction of indignation shows us we have work to do on ourselves. The work is building a healthy ego and letting go of ego inflation. As we escape the bondage of self-importance, we feel the arising in us of a bond to all beings—a spiritual victory.

Early life: Our childhood home was not supposed to be a hard-hat area. Distressing or abusive events that happened in early life can trigger us, as we saw earlier. We will feel especially wounded by any trigger that taps into what is most unresolved from our interactions with our original caregivers. Someone says or does something that mimics what one of our parents said or did. We are reacting not only to what is happening in the present moment but also to the original transactions with our parent. We are transferring onto people now the feelings, needs, attitudes, and expectations that apply to people in our past. Thus, we see a parental face in the person in front of us. We are reacting as if the parent who triggered us long ago is triggering us again now.

To summarize how we are using the three terms in this section we can say the following: The negative shadow will refer to characteristics and proclivities that we have hidden even from ourselves although they come to the surface from time to time. The inflated ego will refer mainly to an arrogant, self-important, demanding, and entitled manner in our dealings with others. Early life issues are composed of memories and experiences, recalled or unconscious, from childhood. We transfer onto others the expectations, needs, and attitudes that pertain to our parents.

In all three instances, we keep in mind that triggers gain momentum from a *belief* in our minds. When the shadow lurks, we feed it with the belief that only she is like this, not I. When our ego is aroused to a combative, bantam reaction we might be believing, "He thinks I'm stupid and can put one over on me but I'll show him!" A reminder of what happened to us in childhood might be supported by the belief that this parental look-alike will punish us just as Dad did if we don't knuckle under.

Regarding the *magnitude* of each of the three let's use a simple analogy. We know the look and layout of the town we live in. We don't know the vast unvisited territories of the rest of planet Earth. In the same way, we know our basic personality characteristics and quirks but we don't know the vast uncharted terrain of our unconscious. Freud said that our conscious mind is like the tip of an iceberg whereas the unconscious mind is the massive submerged part of the iceberg, the part that's underwater. Within the unconscious are repressed memories and what Carl Jung called our shadow: repressed traits, inclinations, and attitudes.

Likewise, we know our ego can function as the strong center of our choice-making and interpersonal relating. But sometimes we act in ways that puff our ego up. For instance, with a healthy ego we can strongly assert our rights. Yet, sometimes we become stuck in a dogged sense of entitlement that comes across as arrogance. That style of ego interferes with healthy relating. So on occasion, or often, we find out that our ego can become dysfunctional and unappealing.

Regarding our childhood experiences and how they impact our attitudes and relationships in the present, there is no doubt that we know only a small amount of it. We keep discovering new memories and realizations that show how subtly and pervasively our early life continues to affect us.

Thus, in all three areas there is, relatively speaking, a town-sized region of what is known and a planet-sized region of what is unknown, though our work on ourselves can certainly help adjust the sizes somewhat. Yet, keeping the basic limitation in mind, we can now look, as intently as we can, at how our shadow, ego, and early life figure into our trigger points. Since no-knowing is actually spacious, we will be eager to open to it.

Our first practice is simple. Whenever we are triggered, upset, we can ask ourselves if one or more of the three mind-sets—our shadow, our ego, our early life issues—are being activated. This will take some spelunking since each of them is so perplexing. Using an acronym helps us remember how to do this check-in: We "S.E.E." what is going on with us. When we check in to which of these has been stirred, we often find it is two or all three. When we are triggered or upset, when something sticks in our craw, we tick down the list and ask ourselves the following questions:

- Am I seeing my own shadow? Do I do the same thing he is doing? Am I looking into a mirror that shows me my hidden self? What in him or in how he is acting signals something unacknowledged in myself?
- Is my inflated ego being wounded? Am I thinking, "How dare she not honor my greatness, not acknowledge my entitlement to special treatment?" Is she getting away with something I can't do anything about or can't get away with too?
- Does this remind me of an early life experience? Am I hearing my mother's or father's voice? Am I putting their faces on this innocent bystander? Am I back in my childhood home?

When we are triggered, we can ask ourselves, "What part of my fear or anger or sadness reaction is about what just happened and what part is trigger energy—that is, what is activated by my shadow or my distressed ego or my early life issues?"

Fortunately, we also have three resources to help us handle the three targets: befriending the shadow, letting go of ego, working through transference by grieving past hurts. Let's look at practices for each of the three:

Befriending Our Shadow

When we befriend the shadow, we trace our projections onto others back to our own issues and traits. We acknowledge them in ourselves and admit them to the other. We then look for what is creative and useful in them. We are not weeding out or eliminating our "unacceptable" parts but instead accepting them and putting them to better use. For instance, I *admit* I am controlling, name that in myself rather than blame others for how controlling they are. My next step is to look for a better use for my controlling energy. For instance, I can be more efficient, good at follow-up, aware of details, have leadership or coordinating skills—without controlling others.

We keep in mind that no matter how much of our shadow we bring into the open and befriend, there is still more—vastly more than we can ever know. The shadow is our entire unconscious, too big ever to resolve or even open in the course of one lifetime. Yet, we don't need to know it all anyway, only how it is operative in this moment. Being healthy does not mean being perfect; rather, it means continually remaining committed to taking one more step in a healthy direction.

Reducing Our Ego Reactions

When we reduce our ego reactions, we notice our arrogance, our competitiveness, our insistence on being top dog, our being in charge. We admit that we feel entitled to special treatment by others, to be honored as superior and treated that way. We look at how we tend to retaliate against anyone who does not bow to our greatness or who hurts us in any way. We look for the spiritual practices that can help us find the virtue of humility.[*]

The ego does not bend to psychological work alone; it takes

---

[*] For more on this, see my book *You Are Not What You Think: The Egoless Path to Self-Esteem and Generous Love* (Boulder: Shambhala Publications, 2015).

a spiritual awakening. We feel suddenly ready to honor equality rather than domination. We have found the "amazing grace" that saves us from the compulsions of a frantic ego trying to maintain its turf. Another avenue to healing opens when we are given a comeuppance, especially by someone we think is below us, and our ego is totally deflated. This time instead of retaliating or re-inflating we take the opportunity to learn a lesson and become more modest, less pretentious.

We do not forget that no matter how much we tame our ego to make it functional there will always be flare-ups of ego inflation because the ego is a much bigger animal than anyone can ever fully tame. We don't rebuke ourselves for that. We only become more humble about our inadequacies, and that makes us more lovable. Then others too help us let go of ego.

Working through Our Transferences

In order to work through our transferences, we look deeply into what happened to us in childhood. We use our inner resource of grieving to process and resolve our ancient hurts. This leads to letting go of resentment toward our parents. Such letting go is the pathway to freedom from transferring resentments onto others. We also do not transfer onto others a demand or expectation that they fulfill the needs our parents failed at. This grief and letting go is a lifetime work but it is very doable and certainly necessary if we are to have healthy relationships.

We remain aware that no matter how much work we do on ourselves, how much exploration of our past we engage in, even with the best state-of-the-art therapy we will never know all that happened to us, all we felt, all we missed. We will also never see all the cunning ways childhood still influences our life and relationships. Nor do we need to. We can live a satisfying life just knowing a little more with each passing era. Yes, we do evolve and become less controlled by our past and the triggers it provokes.

The following outline may help us understand why we take a sudden like of or dislike to someone, which are both examples of triggering:

	I LIKE YOU	I DISLIKE HER OR HIM
SHADOW	I find in you a welcoming of who I am.	She brings out a part of me I do not want to believe is in me.
EGO	I feel no competition or sense of threat.	I instantly want to engage in one-upmanship, put her down, or show her up.
EARLY LIFE	You remind me of a family member whom I cherish.	I feel like I am with a family member with whom I have had difficulties, discomfiting feelings, unresolved conflicts.

The three origins and resources also work in reverse. Other people can be triggered by these same three influences in their dealings with us. Our partner, for instance, might be triggered when we bring her face to face with her own shadow by our behavior toward her. Our ego might be competitive, so we activate a reaction of competitiveness in the other person's ego. We act like a parent and our partner at home or fellow worker on the job has a transference reaction to us. In these instances, all we can do is ask the other how what we said or did affected him. If it is a relationship of trust, we can inquire about the three origins—but very carefully. Our question can come across as a judgment rather than a sincere attempt to find our common truth and work on it together. We are in sensitive territory so we have to tread lightly indeed. Lawrence Durrell, in his novel *Balthazar*, wrote: "It should have the curvature of an embrace, the wordlessness of a lover's code . . . as easy to grasp as, say, an act of tenderness . . . a relationship so delicate that it is all too easily broken by the inquiring mind."

Now we can trek into a deeper dimension of this topic. When we stay with the practice of checking in with ourselves about the three main origins of our triggers, we notice something immensely enlightening: Each of the three can be a darkening screen we use to defend ourselves against a direct gaze at reality:

- The shadow creates a lens of projection. We humans see one another not as we are but as we project.
- The ego is a lens of entitlement. We see each other in accord with what we demand of one another.
- Early life becomes a lens of transference. We put our parents' faces on innocent bystanders in our life story.

As long as our shadow or ego or early life is up and running, we don't see the bare bold reality of what is happening inside us. We don't see what we really want, who we really are, who others are, what is really happening. When we finally glimpse what is actually happening within us, by recognizing the shadow, ego, or early life element, the issue is not such a big deal. Our reaction vanishes quickly.

I have personally experienced this, and it has been enormously liberating. I think I want a person or group of people to like me, include me, or make time for me. I am also quite certain that I want to spend time with them. I am sure I will feel disrespected if they avoid or exclude me. Then suddenly, in an awakening, I get what is really happening inside me: My ego wants some narcissistic recognition, some assurance that I matter to others—maybe as I wanted to matter in childhood. When I see those two elements—ego and early life—as my real concerns, I immediately understand that I don't really want time with that person or group. I only want the sense of being included. The desire is for ego-fluffing and for getting what I missed out on years before. It is not truly about their approval of me or my wanting their company. In other words, I find out what is really going on within me once the ego and early life issues are removed. It works this way with any of the three origins of triggers we are discussing in this section. All three may be used as buffers against an unobstructed contact with reality. Let's use one more example: Suppose we have a childhood-instigated transference that makes someone quite attractive in our eyes. Once that transference disappears and we see him or her simply as an ordinary person, the attraction fades out fast. The swiftness of the change is the clue to our having landed on our own reality.

Transference gains such a powerful hold on us precisely because it remains unconscious. This is why we find release so quickly when we become conscious of what is really going on, when we see, at last, whose face is really in front of us. We then understand what has been happening. Yet, we can end the game. In this process we might come to realize, for instance, how we are still trying to make our parents love us. We come to see how deep our wound is, how profound our ancient longing is. We know our work is to grieve more of our past. We will then feel compassion for ourselves *and* our parents. Soon we notice we are less vulnerable to the trigger. We might even see the droll quality of the game we have been playing with someone who never guessed what we were up to. We know we got it right because all the fears and plans to manipulate the other ended overnight once we caught the demon red-handed. We know we have forded the ancient stream when we can smile, shrug good-naturedly, let go, and move on.

This also applies to the forced ending of an intimate relationship. When we truly grieve and let go of the partner who no longer wants us, we notice we no longer obsess about her every minute of the day. Letting go reduces her size in our psyche. She will not be taking so much room in there as she was wont to do. That is the result of—or reward for—letting her decision no longer trigger us so much. The triggering ends when the obsession ends. Letting go is indeed advantageous since it is simultaneously a release from being triggered.

We only see reality—or one another—in the moments when the three veils have been pulled away. Then the house of cards composed of triggers and reactions collapses on its own. Without the foundations of shadow projection, ego aggrandizement, and early life transference our habitual, conditioned constructions of reality and relationships will surely fall. In the newly opened space, I see you and you see me. *Was a direct panoramic view of reality what I feared all along? Have I built shelters that guard me from being nutritiously rained on by the real me or the real you? How fascinating that I thought I knew so much about me and you but actually had so much more to learn about both of us.*

PRACTICES THAT INCREASE OUR PERSONAL INNER RESOURCES

In this chapter we have explored specific practices to deal with triggers in general. Then we found practices that help us handle three mind-sets that may lurk behind our triggers. Now we round out our treasury of resources by finding ways to enrich the human resources available to all of us. We will do this again with regard to relationships in chapter 7 and then with regard to spirituality in chapter 8.

Paths to Deepening Ourselves

Initiatory painful experiences that we allow, feel fully, and learn from are a boot camp just for us. This is the equivalent of "doing the work": addressing, processing, and resolving present problems, concerns, and painful experiences rather than letting them pass through us unexamined. What makes a soap opera superficial is that nothing is ever processed and resolved. Each chapter opens a new chapter without a full resolution and a completion—the process that would allow for deepening.

As we mature, we come to accept the legitimacy of the deep hole in our psyche and we cease trying to fill it with people, work, food, alcohol, and other distractions. This radical assent is an unconditional yes to the fact that there is an existential emptiness that is common to all of us earthlings. We all find ourselves sometimes lost in a void-of-meaning inside us. That void has other names; it might also be called: openness, fullness of possibility, self-discovery.

We can assent to that desolate place as a fitting feature of our inner landscape—just as we assent to the legitimacy of the Grand Canyon with no attempt to fill it. If the earth reflects our human nature, an unfillable hole must be as important to our inner ecology as it is to the planet's ecology. If I were to descend into the Grand Canyon, I would want to stay there long enough to explore the flora and fauna. Why can't I treat my own inner Grand Canyon with the same fearless curiosity? The Grand Canyon does not tell us that something is missing, only that not everything has to be filled.

The result of deepening is that our psychic dimensions expand, and we become better equipped to activate our potential, a central inner resource. Rainer Maria Rilke refers to this beautifully in a 1914 letter to Magda von Hattingberg as "the boundless resolve, no longer limitable in any direction, to realize one's purest inner possibility."

Serenity, Courage, Wisdom

The affirmation used by twelve-step programs—a prayer originally written by the Lutheran theologian Reinhold Niebuhr—can, for our purposes, be phrased this way: "May I have the serenity to accept what can't be changed, the courage to change what is ready to be changed, and the wisdom to know the difference." We are affirming our loyalty to reality just as it is. Sometimes it invites us to a full surrender to what is beyond our control. That surrender gives us serenity. Sometimes it invites us to take action in order to change something, including ourselves. That action is courage. Finally, we are continually asking the universe, Buddha, Holy Spirit (or other power) for the wisdom to know which flag to salute to: Acceptance or Action. We are not only praying to have serenity, courage, and wisdom—those are already and always in us—but we are also aspiring to activate them in the here and now.

We imagine or hope that we can be in full control of all that is changing. Such control, were it possible, would cancel our chance at building inner resources. Our not being in full control is one of the paradoxical ways our psyche helps us find and increase our inner riches. Along these lines, the Roman emperor Marcus Aurelius in his *Meditations* makes a suggestion for dealing with what upsets—triggers—us, based in the precepts of Stoic philosophy. He proposes continually distinguishing what we have control over and what we do not have control over. Then we can find the appropriate path. His suggestion mirrors all three of the elements of the prayer: accepting what we cannot change, changing what we can, wisely knowing the difference.

Strange how we get so attached to what makes no difference.

—Mona Stevens (played by Lizabeth Scott)
in the 1948 noir film *Pitfall*

Yes to What Is

As we saw above, every trigger is a given of life. To say yes to the probability that people will say or do what triggers us is to face life and relationship as spiritually conscious adults. We understand that anything can happen to any of us. We cannot expect a special deal or an entitlement to an exemption. Yes is also the only link between what happens to us and what good we can make of it—that is, as an opportunity for fearless love. Our affirmation or practice is one I use daily: "May I say yes to all that happens to me today as an opportunity to love more and fear less."

This is a willingness to embrace our daily reality with no attempt to evade or deny it. We have become radical realists both psychologically and spiritually. Such a style allows us to have moods and feelings we are not in control of while still feeling safe and secure. Then, what matters most is not whether bad things happen but rather how we keep building the inner strengths that ground and anchor us. Every time we align our minds and feelings to reality, accept its urgent demand for unconditional respect, accommodate its newest challenges, we increase our inner wealth of assets. "Yes . . . and" rather than "Yes, if . . ." turns triggers into resources.

Our happiness and sense of security can't be based on how much we are in control of our lives and relationships. That contradicts the fact of uncertainty. Our happiness and security have to be based on realism: Since anything can happen to anybody our only safety is in saying an unconditional yes to the way the chips fall and then doing our best to make the most of the way they fell. Then we may notice happiness as a by-product of our yes.

Self-Soothing

When we are triggered, self-soothing can be an inner resource that we put into words: "I manage my anxiety. I can wind down from a crisis. I can calm myself." We have it in us do this without having to use drugs or alcohol. Psalm 131 reminds us of this resource in ourselves, "I have calmed and quieted myself. . . . I am content." Contentment with our present reality is precisely how we calm ourselves. Contentment is being satisfied with what is without wanting more and being satisfied with what is not without complaining about it. When Buddhism recommends letting go of craving and clinging, it is offering us the path to contentment.

As we modulate our feelings we find our power to balance and stabilize ourselves. We do not have to fear our feelings or moods. We can realize they do not have to run us. We can manage them rather than be fragmented or devastated by them. (The fact that we have a neocortex assures us we have this capacity.) The techniques are the standard ones we have found in the self-help movement: breathing exercises, Yoga, relaxation techniques, contact with trusted friends, bodywork, self-assuring affirmations, time in nature, and so on.

Simmering

Triggers evoke an instant reaction. If, whenever possible, we pause and don't react but wait a day or two, the delay allows us to gain a much wider perspective—that is, we access our prefrontal cortex rather than react to the messages in our amygdala. We let the event or experience simmer for a while. The rolling boil ceases and the waters become tranquil. We may still be in reaction, but we are not acting on it. We are letting it become lighter, clearer, not so discomfiting. Our ability to shrug things off kicks in. We thereby feel stronger. Triggers hurt because they disempower us. Simmering recollects our powers and applies them to the issue that triggered us. The sense of having what it takes to deal with what happened goes a long way to reducing the impact of that particular trigger in the future.

With the simmering style, we forego the temptation to make big life-destabilizing decisions when a crisis hits (for example, moving out of town because our spouse left us). With patience as our inner resource we wait till the smoke clears and we trust that a flood of new resources will surely flow in.

Staying with Our Feelings

Life has some givens that we all have to face: Things change and end; life can be unfair; suffering is part of everyone's life; our plans can fall through; people are not always loving or loyal. Each of these givens may trigger a painful reaction. Yet each, by a felicitous grace, can also activate an inner resource, a healthy feeling response. Our feelings are resources because they help us work through and resolve a conflicting experience. Indeed, feelings are our tools, always available, to handle what will definitely happen to us in the course of life. Each feeling can be a technology to help us face life's givens, as in the following outline:

TRIGGERS BASED ON GIVENS	UNHEALTHY REACTIONS	RESOURCEFUL RESPONSES: WE LET OURSELVES FEEL . . .
Losses and hurts	Deny them, blame someone	Sadness, which helps us grieve and let go
Injustice and unfairness	Engage in violence or take revenge	Anger that arouses our protest, assertiveness, and commitment to right the wrong
Threats and dangers	Fight, flee, or freeze	Fear that guides us to protect ourselves proportional to the level of danger
Happy events and good news	Expect the worst to follow	Joy that allows us to cherish the experience

When we have spiritual consciousness, the resourceful responses in the right-hand column do not apply to ourselves only. In spiritual consciousness, we are happy when others find happiness. We care about the losses, injustices, and threats that affect others, both our near and dear and all people on our planet. We feel a universal compassion and we respond in the action-style described in the column on the right. One wounded person makes us bleed too. Pope Francis in his encyclical *Laudato Si'* wrote: "Our goal is . . . to dare to turn what is happening to the world into our own personal suffering and thus to discover what each of us can do about it."

Feelings can trigger us to run or hide. But we can always find our resources; our body has not thrown them away. All it takes is sitting in what we feel. When we let ourselves feel the trigger of loneliness, for example, we are building the inner resources to handle it next time. This is the advantage of our practice of mindfulness as "being here now." We do not seek an escape or blame ourselves or others for how isolated we feel. We do for ourselves what Romeo did for Juliet, saying to ourselves, "I still will stay with thee."

Some of us are only fully aware of our inner resources when we are focused on a project or purpose. We don't know how to handle the blank spaces. But we can find an inner resource to help us find contentment during the times when we feel empty and lost. This resource involves staying with ourselves as we go through our lonely time. "Staying with" means showing ourselves the five As, the components of intimate love that represent our earliest needs: attention, acceptance, appreciation, affection, allowing. It also means not jumping to an escape or distraction but simply staying put. "Staying with" is a physical form of self-acceptance.

We may also notice that we easily tap into our resources when all goes smoothly, is under our control—but not otherwise. We can learn to be ready for times when we are not in control. Again, we stay through. When we hit a wall we go to our inner resource of sitting still. We don't try to break through what resists us. We don't even try to break through our own resistance. We call it by name and stand pat. We let it fall of its own accord and in its own time.

Help from the Past and from Our Memories

Past events can trigger us, especially with shame about particular choices we have made. The "past is prologue" means that all that has happened to us, even (or especially) our mistakes, can be called upon as inner resources. All that happens ultimately has value because we can learn from it. Likewise, no matter how bad things are or what mistakes we have made we can turn to inner resources, one of which is "start over." Finally, every event or experience is valuable because each one gives us yet another chance for spiritual practice.

We do not have to be feeling comforted here and now to find comfort. The memory of what worked before can comfort us. We can recall how we felt with someone who really loved us, with whom we always felt safe, who gave us permission to be who we really are. We hear Ralph Waldo Emerson in his Harvard Divinity School address of 1838: "We mark with light in the memory the few interviews we have had with souls that made our souls wiser, that spoke what we thought, that told us what we knew, that gave us leave to be what we inly are." Who tuned into tones in us that had not yet been sounded, notes we never dared to sing aloud? An encouraging practice is to picture these special people in a circle around us cheering us on.

Indeed, all that people say and do has either comfort or challenge in it and both build resources. Comfort keeps us in the container of ease and security; challenge engages our potential to face our dragons in a courageous way.

We also find inner resources when we imitate the resourceful people we have known. We see them showing courage and we affirm that we have that same potential in ourselves. We practice being brave and find we can step up to the plate as they have. Our heroes show us the resources hidden in ourselves.

The Power of Poetic Imagination

Situations or events trigger us. We are then not able to understand them fully. It may help to write a poem or a journal entry focused on a trigger and our reaction. We thereby access our unconscious riches and make a deeper connection with the issue at hand. A poem especially mines the concrete concern and finds gold in it. This staying with a life question until a decision emerges is how a poem can evoke our inner resource of wisdom. Indeed, a practice of writing a poem to process a triggering situation in our lives, or to respond to an event in the news, evokes a dimension that our rational mind will usually miss. Our poem can be a response to questions like these: How do I handle this trigger resiliently? How do I respond to what just happened to me? What do I feel about this political event or person in the news? In spiritual consciousness, we can ask, How can I experience this in the mind and heart of Buddha? This is an example of combining poetry and practice. We all have the ability to do this; practice increases our ability, our resource.

Resources Need Protection

Material riches need guarding. This is why there is a guard on night duty at financial institutions, why there are walls around buildings, why there are safes, lockboxes, vaults. Temples and tabernacles contain spiritual riches. Thus, they too have walls and locked doors. Our layer of skin likewise guards important internal organs in our body. In traditions with a belief in guardian angels, the angels are guarding our souls. Personal riches may also require hiding; we hide our valuables. It does not make sense to keep wealth unprotected. To do so would be a denial of the shadow side of humans, the predatory side we are all prey to.

Inner resources also need guarding at times. We gladly share our resources with those who need them but not in ways that lead to our being taken advantage of. We set and maintain boundaries around our resources lest they be lost. The danger in being codependent is giving so much that nothing is left in us or for us. A codependent person is triggered by others' needs into excessive generosity or self-sacrifice. If he believes he has not given enough or given priority to his own needs, even once, he is triggered into guilt, shame, and fear of rejection by one he "loves so/too much." When we let others keep crossing the line we have drawn, the line fades away altogether. Then we have nothing left of ourselves or of our adult relationship. We need to protect our valuables, our inner resources, so they can continue to serve us and those close to us.

Self-discipline is a way of protecting our goals in life. There is a part of me that does not obey me. I make choices that can harm my health or self-esteem. Yet at another level, I don't want to keep doing what hurts me. I can turn to an inner resource we all have but one that atrophies when we don't use it: discipline. This does not mean repression; it only means letting go of our resistance to our evolutionary drive to grow and thrive. In mindfulness, I can, in addition, notice the health-negating urges without having to act on them.

William James wrote in "Talks to Teachers on Psychology and to Students on Some of Life's Ideals": "Every good that is worth possessing must be paid in strokes of daily effort. By neglecting the necessary concrete labor, by sparing ourselves the little daily tax, we are positively digging the graves of our higher possibilities." We don't have to reject this statement as an old-fashioned work ethic. We can see it as encouragement to open to our richest potentials. We can frame our idea of discipline as meaning willingness to open to all that we are. Discipline is then the reasonable cost of being all we can be. Discipline is the resource in us that keeps us on track in our magnificent human task to keep on evolving.

FOUR

THE SADNESS TRIGGER

If I defer the grief, I will diminish the gift.
—Eavon Boland, "Pomegranate"

The three most common feelings that arise in our reactions to triggers are sadness, anger, and fear—the main feelings in grief. In this and in the next two chapters we explore these emotions and find the resources to move through them in healthy ways. Indeed, we are not on track when we try to get rid of distressing feelings. We can hold these feelings in ways that foster growth. To "hold" means to experience something fully without becoming overwhelmed or diminished because of it.

It is a given for all of us that life and relationships will toss us losses, endings, disappointments, deficits, deprivations. Each of these, like all the givens to be expected in a human life, becomes a trigger into the healthy response of sadness. This feeling is a built-in technology, an inner resource designed to help us deal effectively with these triggering events. When we let ourselves be sad, we live through our experience of being bereft. The result is that we can get on with our life—that is, we continue on our journey toward lively wholeness.

Throughout this book we distinguish limbic reactions from cognitively based regulation of them. The prefrontal cortex is instrumental in regulating our sadness. It is also, however, used to suppress our sadness. As healthy adults, we choose regulation over suppression.

The word "emotion" means "moving out of" in Latin. Sadness is an emotion. We feel sadness coming on; we allow it to have its full career in our body-mind. We do this when we shed tears, tell the story of our loss, let ourselves mope around as long as we need to. Gradually, our sadness reduces and then releases. Our sadness, like all feelings, arcs over a bell-shaped curve from arising to cresting to declining. This is how it moves through us rather than be bottled up inside us. When we do repress our sadness, we might be vulnerable to depression. Then we find ourselves stuck in an inner vacancy that seems to be inescapable. We cannot feel happiness; we lose interest in our life goals; we slow down in all our activities; we fall into despair. Our levels of serotonin and norepinephrine reduce so much that neural information fails to come through. This is a type of depression based on events that are not processed with the healing experience of sadness. There is also a chemical depression that can last for years, irrespective of events, and for which medication may be an important resource.

Regarding repression of our emotions, we recall that loss automatically triggers sadness, injustice automatically triggers anger, threat automatically triggers fear. When we repress these healthy responses, we interrupt a natural sequence. We lose our chance to ride the arc of an event and to experience its consequent feeling. We forfeit our opportunity to work through what has happened and find closure. Repression is not just part of depression; it blockades us on our heroic journey.

GRIEF ABOUT WHAT WE MISSED EARLY ON

When losses happen, our grief includes being sad that something is gone, angry that it was taken away, and afraid that we will not survive without it. This applies not only to losses of what we had but also to missing out on what we needed and did not receive. For instance, in early life we brought our needs to our parents who, we hoped, would respond with resources, fulfillments of our needs. If they did not do this, we instinctively knew we were not getting what was coming to us. We felt this in one of two ways. It was a deficit—that is, a lack of fulfillment because our parents did not have it to give. Or, it might have been a deprivation—that is, they were holding something back from us that they could have given to us. In either instance, we felt grief.

When the five *As*—attention, acceptance, appreciation, affection, allowing—were not forthcoming we had reason to grieve. But, instead, we might have blamed ourselves, believed that there was something wrong with us. In our adult life we come to see that it was not about that. It was always about the given that some parents don't or can't come through as we need them to. It was always about our path of mourning for what was missing and our giving the five *As* to ourselves as we grew into adulthood. In that self-nurturant style, we were readying ourselves to receive the five *As* from a partner in a healthy adult relationship.

A practice that helps us grieve our losses, hurts, and misattunements from childhood begins with attention to early memories. We use a memory as a cue to the practice: We summon up the three feelings in grief whenever a memory arises of how our caregivers did not come through for us or how they hurt, abandoned, or disappointed us. We can ask ourselves the following questions in an immediate response to the memory, pausing after each, noticing our sensations and feelings:

- How did that sadden me? How am I still holding the sadness now? Where did I feel it in my body then and now?
- How did that anger me? How am I still holding the anger now? Where did I feel it in my body then and now?
- How did that scare me? How am I still holding the fear now? Where did I feel it in my body then and now?

As we progress in this exercise, we are no longer at the mercy of disturbing memories. We are placing them in the container of grief. In other words, we are processing them, not just stacking and storing them in our minds and bodies. We are not hoarding memories; we are making room for them to flow through us like lightning through a lightning rod. They then go safely to ground, that is, back to the earth. We are relocating our painful memories into a healing context. In the neuro-scientific style, we are moving them into a remedial practice. We are taking advantage of what in neuroscience is called "reconditioning," taking an old habit and reworking it. We thereby construct new neural pathways in our brain so that a memory is expanded into a liberation from the hurt it reminds us of. The three feelings, experienced over and over, will gradually give us a sense of completion. The practice helps us foster trust in our bodily timing, another exquisite resource within. If this practice, or any practice in this book, restimulates trauma, we do not continue to use it or we find a way to soften it so that it is endurable.

Our grief practice helps us deal with three givens of life that might also have been features of our childhood: loss, injustice, threat. Sadness is our built-in resource for handling what we experienced as deficits and losses. Anger is displeasure at what we felt was unfair to us in how we were treated. Fear signals danger or threat and activates our resource of self-protection and self-safety, what we are doing in this practice.

An avoidance of grief about what was missing from our childhood home might sound like this: "If I can find someone now to give me what was missing in childhood I don't have to grieve not getting it back then." We might direct this need or demand to an adult partner or even to our parents, now our fellow adults. Most of us have found out that does not work. The only path through is the journey we take on our own, the journey from encapsulation in childhood to liberation into adulthood.

We might also avoid grief by holding onto grievances against our parents or others. In healthy psychological development, however, we let go of the grievances themselves but experience our grief feelings of sadness, anger, fear.

We eventually come to understand a great irony: how little it would have taken to satisfy our need for love! We could have lived for ten years on one caress from Dad. But he just could not or would not bestow even that. There is grief in this for ourselves and for our parents too. When we grieve the past and let it go we finally access the central inner resource that makes us adults, the ability to parent ourselves. It was always in us; now we put it to use and there is someone to hold and protect us and no one left to blame.

Finally, we remind ourselves that any grief process involves a profound and thorough acceptance of the givens of loss, change, hard knocks, unwelcome events, and endings in our human story. We grieve, let go, and say yes to what has been and what is. This is an unconditional yes: no fault, no blame, no protest. Processing, whether it be of grief or resolution of a conflict in a relationship, finds closure only in a final and abiding yes to bare, bald, bold reality: "This happened. It is the way things go sometimes. My only response now can be surrender to this fact. When I finally allow myself to say yes I notice a deeper-than-ever letting go happening within me. It comes with aligning myself with reality rather than wishing for what could have been or regretting what has been. I have found serenity by accepting what cannot be changed." We find a profoundly spiritual suggestion in *The Rubaiyat of Omar Khayyam*: "End in what All begins and ends in: Yes!"

> It's the great mystery of human life that old grief passes gradually into quiet tender joy.
>
> —Father Zossima in Fyodor Dostoyevsky's *The Brothers Karamazov*

MOURNING A DEATH

The passing of someone who matters to us is the most impactful of all triggers. We feel lost in reaction to a loss. In our bereavement, mourning because of a loss, we certainly need—and have—inner resources to call upon. Throughout this book we have referred to processing our experiences. "Processing" means letting ourselves feel fully. Processing is coping, managing and surviving a traumatic event.

Yet, the feelings that come up when we lose someone are often inaccessible at first. We are numb for a while. Our body is wisely preventing our feelings from flooding us. It knows how to grieve little by little or just enough so that we can survive our loss. Denial helps us not let in the full brunt of the desolating loss too fast. This is disbelief, shock, lack of clarity about what exactly happened. All of this is normal. We have to be very patient with ourselves. Mourning takes time and we don't know how much. Our first step in bereavement is to trust our body to show us the path through, in any form it chooses and as long as it needs to. We can trust that the path can escort us, however circuitously, out of our labyrinth of pain.

We can't expect to breeze through grief with our full cadre of mental powers. We are at the mercy of moods that shift constantly. All of this is to be expected. The reaction to most triggers is one or two feelings or actions. The reaction to death is much more complex. It happens in zigzag ways, in phases, ever surprising us with its levels of intensity, its inscrutable timing, its power to destabilize us—whether briefly or for a longer period than we thought possible. Here, too, we have to trust that all that is happening is part of the processing—that is, part of the healing. Our body-mind is trying to absorb a deprivation it was not expecting and for which it will never have enough practice. Mourning is a signature experience, unique to each person—and at each loss—in form, duration, and impact.

Mourning harpoons us physically, psychologically, and spiritually. Physically we may experience tears or collapses at odd times, tiredness, weight changes, insomnia, a reduction in our immune response. This is why it is important to eat and exercise even though we may lose our appetite or not feel like engaging in activity.

Psychologically, we feel sadness that someone is gone. We are angry that he or she was taken from us. We are afraid of the emptiness we will feel now that we are bereft of the one who was such a crucial part of our circle of life companions. We experience guilt that we did not do enough, regret for all the times we did not come through for the one we lost.

Other psychological features of grief can include ongoing anxiety, a lack of energy, thoughts of harming ourselves (including suicidal thoughts), obsession with mental images or memories about our lost loved one. All this is totally natural and not a sign that we are inadequate or that we don't have enough faith or a good enough spiritual practice. Indeed, spiritually, we may find ourselves in a void: We may experience no comfort from our faith or from our spiritual practices. Yet it is crucial to stay with our practices in any case.

Our resources when we are grieving are both internal and external. Internally we acknowledge and talk about our pain. We let ourselves look vulnerable, not try to look strong. We accept the full spectrum of our bewitching moods and bewildering feelings. Externally, we seek support and presence from those we love and respect. We are willing to try therapy if necessary and when we are ready. We remember we are actually being strong, not weak, when we look for help. Indeed, we have become truly unassailable.

It is also important to realize that we do not have to talk about our loss all the time. Just being present with those we love gives us consolation. They can't take away our pain but they can walk beside us as we trudge through the valley of the shadow of death.

WHEN OTHERS ARE SAD

We sometimes encounter sadness in a friend or family member. Our mirror neurons can make our face look as sad as the face of our unhappy friend. We feel with her. Our resource is compassion, the spiritual practice that helps us and others. We show our compassion by understanding rather than judging. We appreciate how it feels to be grieving, especially since we have grieved so often in our own lives. Likewise, we do not give advice or try to console someone with platitudes.

Our reaction of empathy toward someone we know leads us to the compassionate practice of "staying with." This takes the form first of all of physical presence. Our presence happens with compassion for another's pain when we offer her the five *As* of love— attention, acceptance, appreciation, affection, allowing—each a *practice*:

- We pay *attention* to her feeling and her body language with an engaged focus, and we are free of commentary.
- We *accept* her timing. We do not say, "Snap out of it" or "It's time to move on."
- We *appreciate* that the experience of sadness in someone else is entirely individual. It is not meant to duplicate our own. It has its own rules and path and we respect that difference.
- We show *affection* toward the other in appropriate physical ways—for example, holding, if the other is open to it.
- We *allow* the other to let us know how long and how often we are welcome to visit. We ask her what she needs rather than deciding on our own. We make allowances for miscommunications or failed appointments.

All this represents—and makes present—a caring connectedness with another's pain. Since growing in our capacity to love is our life purpose, compassion is a resource not only to the other but to us as well. And all it takes is presence, being with. In his book *Many Ways to Say I Love You*, Fred Rogers—famous for his children's television series *Mister Rogers' Neighborhood*, wisely says, "At many times throughout their lives, children will feel the world has turned topsy-turvy. It's not the ever-present smile that will help them feel secure. It's knowing that love can hold many feelings, including sadness, and that they can count on the people they love to be with them until the world turns right side up again."

As we grow in spiritual consciousness of our connection to all beings, we can feel sad for people who are affected by disasters or violence. When we watch the news on television, we do not have to be spectators only. We might say a prayer or aspiration for them. The eighth-century Buddhist monk and scholar Shantideva expresses this aspiration in *The Way of the Bodhisattva*: "May those who find themselves in a trackless and fearsome wilderness . . . be guarded by beneficent heavenly beings."

In our loving-kindness practice, which will be described in chapter 5, we extend love to ourselves, to our nearest and dearest, to people who are neutral to us, and ultimately to all beings. We can also allow ourselves to grieve for ourselves, for those we love, and yes for all beings who suffer losses and who are hurt or violated. Our empathy extends without limit.

Avoiding Our Grief

Mourning is realism. We feel grief because we have not escaped the reality of an ending. Most of us are adept at avoiding that process, however. Five common ways that we avoid grief are by redirecting our reactions, toward revenge, regret, off-loading, the disregarding of boundaries, and indifference. Let's take a look at each of these.

1. Revenge

A reaction of rage can be a dodge of mourning. A reaction of revenge may likewise cloak our grief. In *Troilus and Cressida* by Shakespeare we hear, "The hope of revenge shall hide our inward woe." A loss feels incomplete, imbalanced. Our most primitive way of resetting a balance may seem to be retaliation. We tell ourselves we were hurt so we will hurt back. Then the scales will be set aright again. But this cancels our natural and necessary mourning about our loss. We imagine that if we get back at someone, we will feel better. That "better" is the equivalent of being deluded into thinking we are "better off" because we have avoided the pain of grief. In reality we have lost an opportunity for closure in the way the body is equipped to find it.

We always keep in mind that retaliation is the favorite sport of ego. Revenge is not then ultimately about righting a wrong. It is also, as we will see in the next chapter, the angry ego's way of salving its indignation.

Grieving without needing to retaliate may be especially difficult for men, who so often have been taught not to cry. So many of us men gradually became afraid of our own sadness. The conditioning drilled into us about what is masculine—revenge—and what is not—weeping—remains in us for a lifetime. But we can work on letting that attitude fade out and letting our grief stand forth. This means allowing ourselves to be fully who we are in response to loss, allowing ourselves to visit the milder climates of humanness where tears are granted entry. Allowing is one of the five *As* of self-love.

2. Regret

Feeling regretful is another way we might be avoiding the full experience of our grief. We may obsess about a recent triggering reaction, bargaining with ourselves about how we might have done something differently so as to achieve a better result. We fall into regret instead of stepping into appropriate grief. Regret is grief that never resolves itself. Instead we spin our wheels in self-pity or self-blame. Regret is a sign that we are not forgiving ourselves and moving on. Since a journey, going on, is built into every one of us, regret is therefore a danger to our evolving as full-on adults. We work with regret by moving past the story of our mistakes to the feelings awaiting closure.

We might be triggered into shame about a choice we have come to regret. The origin of the trigger might hearken back to childhood. We might have been shamed, punished, or rejected for doing what a parent dubbed wrong or bad. If we knew that what we did was not wrong or bad, no trigger resulted. But if we interiorly agreed with the remonstrance, we may now still be triggered into shame. We react by shaming ourselves, another form of regret: "Why did I do what I did?" "How could I make such a mistake?" "How could I be so dumb?" Those are the exact words we used in childhood and we now hear ourselves saying them to ourselves once again. How much of our regret is unresolved grief from our home in a shanty town of long ago?

Pierre Teilhard de Chardin, in his essay "The Cosmic Life," wrote: "I bless the vicissitudes, the good fortune, the misadventures of my career. I bless my own character, my virtues, my faults, my blemishes. I love my own self in the form in which it was given to me and in the form in which my destiny molds me." This is what we can sound like when we forgive ourselves rather than hang out with regret. Ironically, feeling our sadness leads to letting go of it, and then self-blame goes too. We are more likely to forgive ourselves when we have acknowledged our sadness and have let ourselves feel it fully.

We can use an example of how this happens. We are letting ourselves feel our grief about how others have hurt us. Gradually, we feel a shift into letting go of blame, resentment, and the need to retaliate. Letting go of those three *is* forgiveness. When we apply this model to ourselves, we likewise see what self-forgiveness is. We are feeling our sadness and as it is resolving itself it works as a solvent. It washes away our self-blame, self-hatred, and any need to punish ourselves—that is, to engage in self-retaliation. Now we have forgiven ourselves and we can move on. Forgiveness of others or of ourselves does not mean excusing. It means letting go of the rancor we have held inside for too long. We know we have grown up when we notice an indelible trust of ourselves that has survived all the graffiti the inner critic has scratched onto the walls of our psyche.

As an aside, mention of the inner critic brings to mind a humorous irony. If the inner critic says we are stupid and we believe that about ourselves, we are thereby acknowledging that there is an insightful evaluator in ourselves. Thus, belief in the verdict of the inner critic that we are stupid coexists with a salute to what in ourselves is actually intelligent, worth listening to, the very opposite of stupidity! We can notice this contradiction with a smile and that goes a long way to free us from self-loathing.

3. Off-Loading

We sometimes try to rid ourselves of some of our grief by getting others to feel it with us or instead of us. We might do off-loading of our own grief by telling the story of our loss to others so that they can cry for or with us. We may tell our story with a dramatic flourish to garner the other's full attention. We count on the empathy of someone else as a pathway into that person's implicit agreement to take on some of our suffering. We thereby off-load stress from our own bodies into the bodies of others. Shakespeare's character Desdemona describes this process in *Othello*:

> He hath left part of his grief with me,
> To suffer with him.

Sometimes this sharing is healthy. Grief has a shareable dimension. This is why funerals are so useful in expressing and getting through our grief. We are surrounded by others who loved and were loved by our lost loved one. We mourn together and that lifts some of the weight from our hearts. Likewise, when any loss occurs we tell the story over and over to reduce the impact of the grief. All this is how grief moves to closure.

Off-loading is not the same as sharing grief. Off-loading involves shifting some of our own distress onto someone else. This can be motivated by a doubt of or a refusal to access our own inner resources to contain and survive a loss. We look for others whom we consider stronger than we to shoulder some of our pain for us. We place our cross onto the shoulders of a bystander in our story.

We might also become the target of off-loading. Some of us easily fall for it when others tell us their dramatic story of woe about what is happening in their relationship or about a loss of some kind. We feel sympathy, but our involvement may end up being a form of codependency in which we become enmeshed in another person's issue. Then we might be triggered into becoming a rescuer. The problem with this is that the off-loader does not then do her own work. We are making it less likely that the storyteller—who may need to become a client in therapy—will find the help she needs. In other words, we are enabling someone to avoid the appropriate processing of her grief. A friend can be a therapeutic companion but not a therapist.

4. Disregard of Boundaries

When we present a need to someone and she says no to us, the appropriate response is sadness. We are losing our chance to find the fulfillment we so longed for. Most of us, however, immediately occlude our grief about this lack of fulfillment with blame of the other. We say she is withholding, ungenerous, because she is unwilling to give us what is important to us—she is not there for us when we need her. We grieve not getting what we wanted.

The alternative might be pushing to get what we want, insisting on it. We sometimes do not respect boundaries (the boundary here taking the form of the other's right to refuse us). We refuse to take no for an answer. We demand instead that the other come through for us in precisely the way we want. Thus, another hideout from sadness is indignation that we did not get our way.

We might then take the no to be a call to arms. We resent the other, believing we have the right to retaliate when she asks something from us. This style subverts trust. Showing we are saddened by a partner's or friend's response, by contrast, demonstrates our vulnerability, which fosters the other's trust in us. We are then more likely to hear a yes in the future, though that is not our motivation. Once we make the decision that we will be transparent about our feelings, no matter what, we find that sense of courage is the only reward we long for. This courage is liberation from the power others have to trigger us so much.

5. Indifference

We sometimes misunderstand Buddhist teaching. We imagine that if we were enlightened, we would not feel sadness about losses. Endings would be much easier for us to handle. But that extreme stoicism and indifference would be inhuman. Enlightenment is the expression of our inner wholeness. That means allowing the full spectrum of human experience, as part of which feelings are a necessary feature. As social beings we are intimately connected to others. We need one another for survival. We love one another to express our connection in a caring—and joyous—way. A loss ends a connection at least palpably. That matters to beings like us who thrive on a life of collaboration and sharing. Our sadness is our way of showing the importance of our connections.

The Japanese Zen master Shaku Soen was openly weeping over the death of someone close to him. A bystander mocked him, saying, "You are supposed to be beyond reacting to the givens of life and death." Shaku responded: "It is precisely by allowing my natural reaction of grief that I go beyond my grief." The words "go beyond" signify the transcendent—here we are in the spiritual realm. It is certainly a delight to realize that what is natural to us heralds what is supernatural in us.

TEARS IN OUR MORTAL STORY

These poppy petals:
So calmly
Do they fall.

—Ochi Etsujin

In the *Aeneid* by the Roman poet Virgil, the hero Aeneas visits a temple of Juno in Carthage. He comes upon a mural showing events in the Trojan War. In the mural he sees his lost companions in the bloody battles in which he fought. Aeneas cries out, "Sunt lacrimae rerum"—which the Irish poet Seamus Heaney translates to mean "There are tears at the heart of things." There is a sadness built into human experience because all is transitory.

Buddhist teaching describes impermanence as one of the "marks of conditioned existence." Impermanence reflects a central given of life that there will be changes and endings, the ushers of grief. No one can escape meeting them. No one has been granted an exemption from losses. No one can say, "That can't happen to me." All of us are subject to the same unpredictabilities. Certainty is an attempt at permanence, but it is doomed to fail. Indeed, permanence itself contradicts the evolutionary impulse in us and in all things. Only impermanence can accommodate the dazzling vicissitudes of our ever-evolving world.

All of us sometimes feel unsafe. Total safety is also an attempt at permanence. Grieving our losses, allowing our uncertainties and insecurities, escorts us to the all-liberating yes. *Once we truly and radically accept the teaching on impermanence, grieving becomes a spiritual practice.*

The story about Aeneas took place in the temple of the queen of the gods while Aeneas was being given hospitality by Dido, the queen of Carthage. Thus, the experience of impermanence happens for the hero in the context of comfort from the divine feminine and from feminine powers. He felt his pain in the arms of empowering feminine forces. This is where we too find a holding environment in our own grief. In the supporting and strengthening embrace of the divine feminine we find it easier to say yes to the way things are, to the endings no matter how abrupt, to the losses no matter how unfair.

Aeneas noticed that there are tears everywhere. Once we see that the sadness in us is in all of Mother Nature too, we find the deepest solace of all—accompaniment by all that is. That sense of intimate oneness marks the end of our isolation, of the isolation that makes a loss so terrifying. Instead we know we are all in this vale of tears together, all of humanity, all of nature. Somehow that makes our yes to endings and changes more bearable and we pronounce it not with a sullen frown but with a smiling shrug, even a reverent bow.

After each seeming death within my mind or heart, love has returned to re-create hope and to restore life. It has, at its best, made the inherent sadness of life bearable, and its beauty manifest. It has, inexplicably and savingly, provided not only cloak but lantern for the darker seasons and grimmer weather.

—Kay Redfield Jamison, *An Unquiet Mind*

FIVE

THE ANGER TRIGGER

My tongue will tell the anger of my heart,
Or else my heart, concealing it, will break.
—Shakespeare, *The Taming of the Shrew*

We suddenly blow up at someone. Our partner—or we—engage in angry outbursts. They are touched off by a minor issue. We realize the immediate situation does not account for the bigness of the reaction. We are in the battleground of triggers.

"Anger" is defined in the dictionary as irritation at unfairness. We react with a distressed feeling, anger, when we are triggered by something that we consider unjust or unfair to us or others. The feeling of anger is normal. It is appropriate to be triggered into an angry reaction when something that we consider inequitable is happening. It is up to us, as we shall see in this chapter, to show our anger in ways that are nonviolent and in control. We want our bid for fairness to be heard. This can only happen when the person we are interacting with can hear our feeling without feeling intimidated. To communicate safely, especially in our close relationships, we call on our resources of respect, self-control, and appropriate expression of heated feelings in either direction. This takes practice, which we will explore in this chapter

Remember that the prefrontal cortex regulates emotion and adjusts it to efficient decision-making. The amygdala goes online when we are triggered into anger. It scans the landscape for threat and activates an anger—or fear—reaction so that we can deal with it effectively. Since the amygdala is also our repository of early feeling-laden memories, we might feel a present threat with the same impact it had when we were powerless children. When this happens, our cognitive processes cannot easily connect triggers to resources, unless we find the mindful calm that anger usually annuls. We find our resources when our mind is mindful again. We can learn that skill.

IS IT ANGER OR ABUSE?

We can distinguish healthy anger—a feeling—from abuse—a theatrical display, a tantrum, losing our temper. The first is always in control; the second goes out of control. It may be hard to believe that we can keep our cool when we are angry, but it is very doable when we practice mindfulness in our daily life. We become adept at experiencing whatever happens, no matter how upsetting, with calm awareness and clarity.

We are responsive to injustice on a bodily and feeling level—that is, we become angry. But we can do so within limits that are assertive toward others rather than aggressive toward them. We express our truth about what they have done in respectful ways. That is assertiveness. We do not cross the line and come at them with threats, name-calling, derision, hostility. That is aggression—what we call abuse.

We sometimes meet up with anger from others, sometimes abuse. Anger, like all feelings, is a form of communication. The abuser, on the other hand, wants to dump on us—not engage in dialogue. Anger informs us, so we greet it with rapt attention. It opens us to dialogue. Abuse is meant to silence us and shut us down. In the assertive anger style, we treat those whose behavior has aroused us as peers, not as targets. Anger honors equality. Abuse treats others as objects of wrath.

We might think we fear anger; actually, we fear abuse. Healthy anger will grab our attention so we participate in the communication. We will listen intently because an authentic feeling engages both our limbic system and our prefrontal cortex. When we are bombarded by abuse that masquerades as anger, only our limbic system responds. Then we are on guard. We rightly fear we might be in danger, that violence might erupt. That sense of threat is the result of intimidation. In this instance it is not really anger coming at us; it is a strategy meant to frighten us. We are triggered into fear and on the defensive. This is because abuse is adversarial and includes ill will, an intent to harm. Anger maintains goodwill while saying "Ouch!" to which we might say "Oops!" This is fearless on both sides, and from such sincere sharing comes conversing—not contesting.

Anger declares the impact of what someone has said or done, declares how we have been triggered by him. Abuse bullies the other rather than opens a portal to more understanding about how our behavior has landed. That understanding does not matter to an abuser; all that matters is his getting his rage out.

In the abusive style, we blame the other; in healthy anger, we take responsibility for our feeling. We see the one who triggered us as a catalyst, as all triggers are, rather than a cause, what triggers are not. We can experience it this way because our anger is directed at what happened, not at how our inflated ego was punctured. Abuse is about an indignant ego; anger is about how we are feeling wounded. Yet, since bruising can be a hazard in any interaction, we can take it as a given for all humans. We are then not ego-indignant and fit to be tied; we are hurt but still able to be open. The inflated ego believes itself entitled to full justification, a style that justifies abuse. The angered healthy ego seeks not self-justification but rather a fair hearing. We are not self-righteous but self-expressive.

The arrogant ego feels compelled to save face by getting back at the one who triggered his wrath. This is a form of alienation, separation, driving a wedge between himself and us. It is the opposite of our natural inclination in evolution, to move toward more and more connection. The abuser moves against others; the angry person moves toward the other. The angry person wants reconciliation, not punishment of the other. The goal is forgiveness, not smoldering resentment. This is why anger can coexist with love but abuse cannot. In anger, we are upset but the connection endures; in abuse, we are upset and the connection is broken. Anger is the shortest feeling; it rises, crests, and reduces within minutes. Abuse, fueled by revenge and grudge, can go on for a lifetime.

Both anger and abuse include grief. In each instance, we are sad and incensed by what has triggered us. In healthy anger, we declare not only how livid we are but also how hurt and sad we are. An abuser is afraid of such vulnerability. She will hide her grief, deny it, mask it with intimidating rage. How puzzling that we use what looks like anger to evade the authentic expression of anger. In healthy anger, we address, process, and resolve our grievance with someone who has triggered us. In abuse, we refuse to do that, preferring a feud.

Although anger and abuse can look a lot alike—for instance, the red face is the same in both—they have some distinct differences: A raised voice shows emphasis in anger. Its purpose is to garner our attention so we can respond. In abuse we hear a screaming voice that is meant to frighten us. The gestures that go with the words in anger are dramatic but in abuse they are menacing or physically invasive. They are not ways of showing a feeling bodily; they are bodily posturings and can even come to blows. Finally, implicit in anger is a request that we change. In the dark side of anger, abuse, we hear a demand that we change or else.

The following outline shows differences between anger and abuse at a glance.

HEALTHY ANGER	ABUSE
Expresses a feeling in an authentic way	Becomes a tantrum in a theatrical way
Takes responsibility for the feeling	Blames the other person
May be expressed with a red face, excited gestures, a raised voice, a sharp tone	May be expressed with a red face, menacing gestures, posturing, a screaming voice, a cutting tone
Says "Ouch!" assertively and respectfully while seeking a dialogue	Is aggressive and adversarial, is an attack based on ill will and with an intent to harm
Communicates, reports an impact, to reach the other	Puts down, bullies, or dumps on the other
Informs the other, creates rapt attention in the other so that we want to have a dialogue	Intimidates, threatens, and attempts to overpower the other so the only safety lies in leaving the premises until things cool down
Is nonviolent, in control, and always shown within safe limits (manages temper)	Is violent, out of control, derisive, hostile, and punitive (loses temper)
Asks for change	Demands change
Recognizes the injustice as reparable	Is resistant to repair
Maintains goodwill at all times	Maintains a mean ill will toward the other
Asks for accountability and amends to clear things up so forgiveness can happen	Seeks revenge, keeps holding something against the other
Seeks mutual transformation	Seeks to justify oneself
Sees the other as a *catalyst* for the feeling	Believes the other is the *cause* of the reaction
Does not believe any provocation legitimates an abusive reaction	Believes a provocation justifies aggression or even violence
Includes grief and acknowledges it	Includes grief but masks or denies it
Shows respect for the other as a peer	Shows contempt toward the other as a target
Aims at a deeper and more effective bond: an angry person moves *toward* the other	Wants to vent the rage no matter who gets hurt: an abuser moves *against* the other
Is brief and lets go with a sense of closure (like a flare)	Is held on to as lingering resentment, hate, grudge, or bitterness (like a smoldering fire)

HEALTHY ANGER	ABUSE
Coexists with love, maintains connection	Cancels the connection
Is fearless	Is fear-based
Is a form of addressing, processing, and resolving an issue with spiritual consciousness	*Is a form of avoiding one's own grief and distress about an issue with a refusal to work things out and thereby to grow spiritually*

THE ANGRY EGO

We have examined how the ego is aroused, triggered by a perceived slight. Now we can look more closely at how the ego is implicated in anger and abuse.

The healthy ego is the mind-set in us that assesses correctly and acts with forethought so that our goals in life can be fulfilled. The inflated ego is the mind-set that operates on arrogance and entitlement. When that is afoot we might be met with abuse rather than healthy anger.

Anger is displeasure at injustice. Yet, beyond the justice issue, we might also react with anger when we become frustrated. Perhaps we expect to reach a goal and do not. Or we expect a reward and it is not forthcoming. We are displeased that we did not receive what we believed we were entitled to. This kind of frustration can be part of a healthy ego response. That happens when we feel the frustration, grieve it, try to deal with it, seek a positive outcome. But when the inflated ego is frustrated it can become mean-spirited—armed and dangerous. In that frame of mind we might turn on those implicated in our frustration. We might blame others for it. We then are expressing not anger but abuse. Anyone will find that frustration-driven approach scary. The fear in that instance incites the other to run. This is often his wisest course of action since abuse can't be reasoned with.

The inflated ego fears losing face because that would result in shame, a feeling it cannot tolerate. Behind the bluster, bravado, and swagger of ego is fear of vulnerability. Most people imagine that anger is the most dangerous feeling to meet up with in others. Actually, it is fear that is most dangerous, because fear is more likely to lead to a reckless reaction—the kind of reaction that becomes abuse. When an ego-entitled person is frustrated in his demands, he is incensed and believes he is justified in showing wrath and even violence. He turns on the one he sees as the culprit with abuse and intimidation. As an example, a driver feels fear because of the immediate sense of danger when he is cut off in traffic. This turns into road rage and he might react in a way that endangers or harms the other driver, or any other drivers, or himself. Road rage is a reaction to the trigger of a perceived insult. It is, in effect, an ego feeling intimidated and taking revenge.

Healthy anger, on the other hand, leads to short eruption and then closure. When we look into the eyes of an abuser, we do not see anger; we see fear. Ultimately, the inflated ego has to be in control because if she does not get what she wants she will have to feel sadness. The prospect of such vulnerability is terrifying. This is the real fear under the hatchet she aims in our direction.

The inflated ego has a sense of entitlement that is beyond the ordinary sense of rights. The healthy ego believes it has rights and is ready to stand up for them. These rights include respect for the given of life that we don't always get what we want. An adult knows that life is not always fair. The inflated ego demands fairness no matter what. An adult has accepted the fact that people are not always loyal and loving. The ego-inflated person demands that everyone be loyal and loving to him—though he is not obliged to be that way toward others. An adult knows that anything can happen to anyone. Ego inflation insists on an exemption from that given—from all of the givens of ordinary life, ultimately. That is what is meant by ego entitlement.

WHY WE FEAR OTHERS' ANGER

As we have been seeing throughout this book, triggers and reactions are two sides of one coin. We can be triggered into anger: An experience of unfairness can be the stimulus; anger can be our reaction. We might also be triggered *by* anger; then our reaction may take the form of placating or avoiding. Both of these are related to fear. What is it about an angry face that scares us? Here are some possible reasons for such a trigger:

- In our childhood we might have seen only abuse. This became synonymous in our minds—amygdala—with anger. This can happen when we had no model of healthy, non-harming anger. If we suffer post-traumatic stress from past abusive experience, we may now be on high alert for the slightest frown that we believe may erupt into danger or harm. We might become people-pleasers in such an instance. We resort to placating rather than speaking truth to power. We are thus afraid of others' anger and even more afraid to show our own anger.

- Anger feels like opposition. This is the equivalent of distancing, separation. Since we are social animals, we fear being exiled from the herd. We fear being left on the hillside while the herd continues on its journey. People fear abandonment more than any other psychological predicament. Exclusion means not surviving. We might read anger, no matter how sanely and safely expressed, as placing us in serious peril of isolation. Then to please is to live; to displease is to die.

- We have seen irritation magnify itself and erupt into abuse. We may sometimes have been the victims of it. We may, therefore, now do all we can to smooth the waters, to concede, smile winsomely, attempt to curry favor. We might then grovel, be at the beck and call of the person whose anger terrifies us. We lose our sense of our own power and self-respect. We then become passive yes-persons, rather than strong sailors who take the chance of rocking the boat.

- We may hold back from expressing our anger because we fear that if we do express it the other person will not like us anymore. We fail to see that healthy anger ultimately brings people closer together. It is only abuse that drives us apart. Real anger coexists with and enhances closeness. When we can share our displeasure we are sharing our hearts. We are allowing the full range of human feeling, all legitimate in any relationship.

- Fear of anger evokes a trust issue. We may fear others' anger because it leads to our feeling unsafe and insecure. When someone comes at us with anger, we want it to happen in an atmosphere of safety and security. In a healthy relationship we can say, "Let's find out what scares each of us and present our anger at one another in ways that avoid that pitfall. Let's assure one another of our safe and secure connection no matter how angry we become."

Some people are afraid to show us their anger directly. They might then engage in *passive aggression*. They do little—or big— things that upset us. Examples are being late for something important to us, forgetting an appointment altogether, making us jealous by their attention to someone who seems like a rival.

When someone shows authentic anger, we feel safe so we stay put: "You are angry now and I will hear you out." But when someone is abusive, our healthy response is to leave the premises: "It seems to me that you have crossed the line and are coming at me aggressively so I will leave now and come back when you calm down so we can have a useful conversation."

We can choose an alternative response to leaving *if we are up to it*. By way of illustration, I offer a memorable example from the sixties era when I worked at an Italian neighborhood counseling center in Boston: A surly guy who had come in off the street was using intimidating words and gestures toward Anthony, a local athlete who helped out at our center. Anthony had no training in counseling, but he responded to the visitor's behavior in a way that was so impressive I still remember his three sentences: "Hey man, I don't want you coming at me that way," he said. "You're scaring me, and I don't like to be scared. Just tell me what you want."

Over the years I have deconstructed Anthony's words: The first sentence sets boundaries without aggressiveness or judgment. The second shows a vulnerability that nonetheless includes strength. The third invites the other person to express his need more appropriately.

I see these three elements—limit-setting, vulnerability, invitation to express a need—as a wholesome combination of assertiveness and nondefensiveness. I suggest this approach now as a healthy response to rage if we have built our assertiveness skills sufficiently to practice it.

Note that Anthony was triggered into fear but did not react either with a bantam ego or with placating. He responded by using (1) nonthreatening directness, (2) not backing down, and (3) creating an opening for effective communication. We need fortitude—and self-respect—for a practice like this. We increase our fortitude and self-respect when we attempt it.

I complete my story by saying that the visitor to our center looked back at Anthony in silence for a long few seconds. Then he did indeed ask for what he wanted, respectfully. It is not a given that such a response from an aggressor is guaranteed. But others' responses to us become less weighty when we feel so good about ourselves for having acted admirably.

If anger that dwells in our heart lies neglected and turns instead to our external foes, we try to destroy them. Seeing that this action is not the solution, let us muster the forces of mercy and love, turn inwards and tame the wild flow of our mind-stream. This is the way of the Bodhisattva.

—Ngulchu Thogme Zangpo, *Bodhisattva Practices*

A NEW WORLD

A new era is upon us. Even the lesson of victory itself brings with it profound concern, both for our future security and the survival of civilization. The destructiveness of the war potential, through progressive advances in scientific discovery, has in fact now reached a point which revises the traditional concepts of war. . . . Various methods through the ages have been attempted to devise an international process to prevent or settle disputes between nations. From the very start, workable methods were found insofar as individual citizens were concerned, but the mechanics of an instrumentality of larger international scope have never been successful. Military alliances, balances of power, leagues of nations, all in turn failed, leaving the only path to be by way of the crucible of war. The utter destructiveness of war now blots out this alternative. We have had our last chance. If we do not now devise some greater and more equitable system, Armageddon will be at our door.

—General Douglas MacArthur, radio broadcast
from the USS *Missouri* after the surrender of Japan,
officially ending World War II (September 2, 1945)

We come into the world not as blank slates but with some settings, some natural instincts, already plugged into our psyches. This human gene pool certainly has breathtakingly positive qualities. For instance, we can find a redemptive value in suffering. We can love one another unconditionally. We can stand up for our rights and the rights of others with courageous bravado. We can find ways to make peace. We can care about ourselves, one another, and the planet. We can be just, and even generous. These are examples of our sterling assets and potentials as human beings, resources we share in the world around us.

Yet, all is not sweetness and light. We remind ourselves that we also have it in us to fall prey to hate or to join a lynch mob. This shows us that there is more inside us than Buddha nature or Christ consciousness. We can't overlook our enduring potential for aggressiveness, what we described earlier as the shadow side of healthy anger. Knowing we have this inclination keeps us on guard over ourselves and encourages us to practice showing gentle love in all our dealings. This is our only defense against the inner and oncoming dark.

Indeed, this gene pool of ours has some serious birth defects. We have a collective shadow side, a penchant toward harming, hurting, engaging in or standing by and allowing evil. This negative shadow energy in us has included, and still includes, war, torture, genocide, hate crimes, revenge, oppression, slavery, greed, abuse of the earth, and myriad forms of violence. In the face of these harsh examples of aggression we can choose goodness and join those who stand up for what is just and beneficial. On the other hand, we sometimes join the evil forces or even persecute those who stand for goodness.

On a collective basis some negative-shadow built-in inclinations are fixed in the structures of our psyche as our human heritage from our ancient ancestors. The settings have evolved over the millennia so that more sophisticated societies can survive. Yet, they remain primitive and fear-based on many levels—for example, in confronting conflict. Let's focus on two of these proclivities toward aggression that are present almost universally in individuals, groups, and societies:

1. Maintaining order by the threat of punishment: In a society, order tends to break down if there are no sanctions in place to maintain it. Most of us seem to need the threat of punish-

ment as a motivation to follow all the rules of society. We also carry over the collective practice of punishment and retaliation into our personal relationships. This is scary since it is how humans may become feral.

2. Forming in-groups and being xenophobic: We know we are evolving toward more connectedness. People do indeed keep forming close bonds within society, but they do so mostly in their own in-groupings—rather than with an embrace of the whole of humanity. We unite with those who are like us or who like what we like. We are intensely loyal to "our own" and tend to disparage or even harm those who are different from us. We join those who think and act as we do; we fear and exclude those who do not.

Spiritual leaders have come along to show us another option, universal love. We need such teachers because otherwise we would have no program to follow but the two fear-based patterns of societal evolution. Thus, when our conscious purpose in evolution is about awakening to our Buddha nature or the Christ within, both the inclinations above can be transformed. We then become deeply humane, not simply human. With a spiritual orientation, we have the option of evolving from the primitive style of punishment and xenophobia to advancing as a society of universal love and caring connection: The negative inclinations are in us and fear brings them out. The positive inclinations are also in us and enlightened awareness brings them out.

With unconditional connectedness as the model of evolution, we emerge as an awakened humanity, one committed to a world of fellowship. We then seek to rehabilitate those who go awry, not retaliate against them. We want the style of reconciliation, not retribution. We feel universal loyalty to a global humanity, not only to our insider group. We look for ways to bring everyone in, not ways to keep some out. Our motivation to be like the caring saints and heroes we admire has superseded our motivation to stay in the perennial primitive pattern. We are then a truly evolved humanity, not simply a herd satisfied with survival no matter who gets hurt.

With nothing going for us humans beyond what survival-based evolution has built into us, there is not much hope for a better world. Yet, since we also have access to grace—assistance beyond ego—we can awaken our growth-based evolutionary impulses. Then optimal connectedness flourishes. It will take a commitment to live the teachings of Buddha, Jesus, Gandhi, the Dalai Lama, for that unity to become visible in our world today. Now we see why:

- When the direction of evolution is persistence in existence, its goal is the survival of those who are fittest for physical and mental maturation—only some of us. This produces the world we have now.
- When the direction of evolution is caring connection, its goal is the survival of those who are fittest for physical, mental, and spiritual maturation—all of us. This can produce a world of justice, peace, and love.

Hope for us and our planet is based on the evolutionary nature of all that is. All is tensed toward growth, has a developmental direction. We build our hope when we enter into the arc of this growth. Such entry is having an evolutionary spirituality. We are not doing spiritual practices to gain merit for ourselves or to be more enlightened than others. Our entire program of spiritual awareness and practice is in the style of loving-kindness, equally oriented to everyone as to ourselves and to those we love personally. We are doing what evolution does: move in ever-widening circles to include all beings and our planet in connectedness and collaboration. We each have a life goal in our relationships, careers, and fulfillment of longings. We all have the same goal in our evolutionary purpose, co-creating a world of justice, peace, and love.

Love is the most universal, the most tremendous and the most mystical of cosmic forces. Love is the primal and universal psychic energy. Love is a sacred reserve of energy; it is like the blood of spiritual evolution.

—Pierre Teilhard de Chardin, *The Spirit of the Earth*

SIX
THE FEAR TRIGGER

Fear is the mind killer. Fear is the little death that brings total obliteration. I will face my fear. I will permit it to pass over me and through me. And when it has gone past me I will turn to see fear's path. Where the fear has gone there will be nothing. Only I will remain.

—Frank Herbert, *Dune*

Triggers often arouse fear in us. Fear is a central obstacle to building and accessing our inner resources. Some fears trick us into believing that we have no inner resources. We can understand why most of us are at the mercy of many, too many, fears. We inherited fear from our ancient ancestors. Only our forebears who had fears survived. For example, people with a fear of snakes lived on; those who were curious died out. Thus, the natural human aversion to snakes is imprinted in us descendants for survival's sake. We will always have such primitive fears, the ones we inherited from our Cro-Magnon ancestors. They reside in our amygdala, the primitive reptilian part of our brain that holds fears from ancient times and from childhood too. In our example, we inherited a realistic fear and caution about what can be truly dangerous. It is also true that the ancestors who had courage in the face of fear, while being cautious too, survived and thrived. We have inherited that balance.

We want to keep our realistic fears. Yet, we also have *unfounded* fears: We imagine a threat where there is none, forecasting or dreading an outcome that will never happen, being scared of things that are not really so daunting. Our goal is not to get rid of fears like these. Our goal is simply not to act on them. We do not have to let them stop us from living in accord with our deepest needs, values, and wishes. We do not have to let them push us into actions that are self-diminishing or self-limiting. When we are strong in this way, we have accessed the courage that is as deeply in us as fear. Believing we are indeed courageous builds self-trust, a central inner resource in the face of any triggering fear.

Unfounded fears thrive on the richness of our imagination. We drum up thoughts that depict the serious consequences that might happen to us because of some triggering event. Most of us are quite adept at imagining the worst in ever more outrageous ways. It is sad to notice how much of our wonderful inner resource, imagination, goes into fueling our fears. So much of that creativity could be invested instead in exciting ideas and extraordinary innovations. Working on letting go of fear is therefore a path to accessing new ways of dressing up our routine lives with newfound courage and kaleidoscopic variety.

When fear dominates us, it short-circuits the full experience of who we are. Fear revokes our freedom to be ourselves. Thus, to fear is to doubt our own power, to stunt it, to crimp our full human stature. We sometimes fear having power, and that disempowers us even further. We believe we have no inner resources—that is, are at the mercy of triggers. Most fear is terror that our carefully constructed and continually refortified citadel of control over our feelings will fall. What we really fear are the uncontrollable bodily sensations and reactions that will accompany *release* from fear—and from trauma too.

When we have focused on being in control of people, feelings, and events we set ourselves up for worry when things happen beyond our control. That worry is the price we pay for all the years of energy we put into making sure we were in control. The alternative attitude is surrender of control. It will be a "yes" to two simple but unwelcome givens: First, we accept the fact that we won't always be able to control outcomes, so it is wise to invest some energy into devising a program for that eventuality—deciding, for instance, "Let the chips fall where they may. I will grieve if I don't like the way they fall and then make the best of the way they fell." Secondly, we can trust that whatever happens offers us an opportunity to love more and fear less. Our program then is simply gratitude.

BOTH DESIRES AND FEARS

Relationships evoke desires. The many kinds of desire fall essentially into two categories. A *single-level desire* is about the object only: "I need a flashlight for my camping trip. I want only that, and I will be satisfied when I have it." Our desire is straightforward and satisfiable. A *multi-level desire* is about more than the stated object: "I need a late-night snack when I am alone and lonely. I am wanting more than what I think I need and then I am not satisfied anyway." (That would not happen with the desire for a flashlight!) Our desire is complicated and unsatisfiable.

With a multi-level desire, we can immediately ask, What are we *seeking* and what are we *avoiding*? Feeling these two at once is also the thing that underlies addiction. We are seeking some form of satisfaction while also avoiding something; we feel desire and fear simultaneously. This is why addiction is so confounding. It mixes fear and desire and thus stymies us.

Let's say we have an addictive desire for sex. It is obsessive and compulsive and has many levels of meaning in our lives. Our healthy ambition is for more than physical satisfaction. We may actually be looking for one or more of the five *A*s—attention, acceptance, appreciation, affection, allowing—our original needs in early life, and the components of love throughout life. For example, we long for fatherly love, a holding presence with the five *A*s, a sense of safety and security. We want a "stay with" experience, which we did not get from Dad. We now look for that kind of love, but through sex rather than in ongoing committed intimacy. When we find it we feel dopamine, the hormone of reward, coursing through us, and that fuels the addictive cycle.

However, our addiction is also about avoidance: we fear the intimate connection that might give us true need fulfillment. We prefer dopamine to oxytocin. We combine fear and desire and *sexualize* our deep and ancient longing rather than trust that we can find it in a relationship. In addition, we might be attracted only to the one who is available for this game of hide-and-seek, the one who has the same agenda we have. He or she is the one very ready to play it all out with us. We dependents and codependents easily find each other.

We thus use sex to get what we seek and avoid what we fear. How? We choose exciting sexual activity instead of contented sexual connection—giving us what we seek but with no need to avoid. We seek adrenaline and excess dopamine, not oxytocin.

Neural plasticity is good news regarding positive change. But when it comes to the release of dopamine, that same plasticity can make us less flexible, less apt to find new ways to think and act. Dopamine is related to reward, pleasure, a sometimes false sense of control and confidence. When we seek it addictively, we foreclose on our chances to move beyond what it offers and get on with life in a more well-rounded way. We are caught in a circular feedback system that freezes our options.

In this example, desire for fatherly or motherly love can also lead us to search for an older man or woman as a partner. We think, "This person I am attracted to will either give me what I seek or reject me, as Dad (or Mom) did or did not." Or we could want a younger man or woman. Then we ourselves become the affectionate father or mother figure: "I show this person what I want rather than get it. Now I get it by giving it." Why seek younger rather than older? It might be because the transaction feels *safer* with someone younger.

Seeing all this in our behavior, our challenge is to have unconditional compassion for ourselves and others. We might also go deeper into our predicament and ask this question: *Do I fear fatherly or motherly love too?*

Finally, acceptance and rejection can be triggers of empowerment or disempowerment of our ego. We feel powerful when we are accepted by someone, which can lead to ego inflation. We feel our power diminished when we are rejected, the experience that can deflate our ego. Now we can understand why rejection harpoons us so hard while acceptance feels so good. In a way, having power is having an identity; without it we are no one. How ironic that letting go of being someone is enlightenment in Buddhism but a frightening loss in the ego's world.

WHEN CLOSENESS IS SCARY

Why is intimacy so scary? It may be because it invites us into fearless vulnerability, fearless surrender of ego, fearless trust even when the evidence is sketchy, fearless letting go of control, fearless willingness to be seen through and through all the way to the bottom of ourselves. We are challenged to reveal all the parts we would prefer to keep hidden and place them in full-frontal view.

Interrelatedness, deep connection, has a comforting ring to it. Yet, it evokes ambivalent feelings in us. Most of us desire closeness and fear it at the same time. We hear of this from William Wordsworth in "Tintern Abbey":

> More like a man
> Flying from something that he dreads, than one
> Who sought the thing he loved.

In intimate relationships it is normal that there be some ambivalence both about closeness and commitment. Thus, we look for loopholes; we fudge here and there. Unconditionality is certainly not possible all the time, only in moments. We may never find the full fearlessness that closeness and commitment ask of us. But we would not want to use this realization to rationalize our fears. We can instead engage in some practices that move us along: We can show more and more transparency in our relationship. We can admit our fears. We can support each other in getting past them. We can open to a little more closeness and a little deeper commitment daily. As the first step toward full relating, we can even give up trying to be perfect.

We find it scary to trust others—although trust is an essential ingredient of loving—because the possibility of betrayal frightens us. Our fear of trusting is also a fear of vulnerability. This can prevent us from accessing the love we long for. How sad that trust, which best expresses who we are—people in connection—can so keenly frighten us at the same time. Our ego is looking out for number one, believing its own interests are all that matter. We then miss the point. We fail to realize that such a fear-based attitude undermines the possibility of achieving the thing that can truly make us whole and happy. When we fear closeness, we become experts at distancing:

I don't show my vulnerability.

That would make me more lovable.

Then closeness would happen.

That is scary.

So my safety consists in not being vulnerable.

I have come full circle back to a closed heart.

In this strange quandary, of wanting and needing what we are also fearing and avoiding, it is understandable that closeness becomes a trigger. The fear might sound like this: "In this relationship, you are demanding what I have feared all my life to give."

Let's look carefully into what may be going on when we fear being engulfed: It can be a throwback to a traumatic experience in childhood when we were overly controlled or patrolled by a parent. It might also be a throwback to how a parent smothered us with invasive affection. We had no way of establishing a boundary, of protecting ourselves. That connection between closeness and powerlessness led to a trigger: We are now triggered into fear by closeness even when it is expressed appropriately, so our reaction is to run from it. Superficially, this may seem like a fear of being engulfed and defending against it. But, more subtly, it can be that we are *using* our fear to keep people away. We might use fear in this way rather than engage in limit-setting, the adult way of dealing with closeness that becomes uncomfortable for us. But if we can be assertive about our comfort zone, we no longer have to keep people away. We can let them know our boundaries directly. We can tell them how much and what kind of closeness works for us. Then we are truly protecting ourselves while still allowing the closeness we long for. We no longer have to use fear as a wall to keep out what we ultimately want.

We might also be triggered by the prospect of making a commitment. We might be triggered into fear by noticing that a person has committed herself to us. We might feel that puts us on the spot. We might feel engulfed, obliged, indebted—all powerful triggers in any relationship. We fear losing our freedom. Our reactions to such triggers might be to avoid full commitment, to find a way out of the relationship or a way of buffering its impact on us. We are careful not to have both feet planted in the relationship.

In so many relationships there is, for example, a third party, noticed or unnoticed—something going on that prevents or protects us against full commitment. It can be a person, a thing, or an ongoing triggering issue. In each instance, the partners keep themselves one step removed from one another because they have to focus on what is standing between them. That third is a buffer against both closeness and commitment.

Such in-betweens can take many forms: a divorce not yet finalized, a money problem, an addiction, an affair in progress, an unmet need or expectation, a conflict that can't be resolved, a grudge, or a child, parent, or former partner with needs. The third party can also be an unresolved issue from the past of one of the partners—for instance, resentment remaining in a betrayed partner about an affair now long over. That third presence requires so much focus that it becomes, in effect, another member of the relationship. The partners never have to face life only as a couple, a prospect that has become too scary. A presence between partners likewise saves them from having to feel and face that very fear. We may, for instance, use an affair both to avoid closeness—the fear dimension—and to look for it in a noncommitted way—the safety dimension.

The between-presence also serves to make a partner stay longer in a relationship that doesn't really work. The phantom partner—the third party, event, or thing—makes an unbearable life together tolerable: "As long as we are concentrating on our son's addiction we don't have to notice and deal with our own problems." We can't help but notice the similarity between this issue in a relationship and what happens in politics: "As long as we are concentrating on foreign wars we don't have to admit, focus on, and deal with our domestic problems."

Weaponizing is another subtle way of maintaining distance when we fear closeness in a relationship. For instance, Robin has a habit of cutting off communication when Adrian wants to talk. Adrian is willing to overlook this because it gives him ammunition to use later. He can build resentment toward Robin for not listening. He also feels justified in making a unilateral decision and keeping it a secret. Adrian feels justified in this because he figures that Robin will only disregard or discount his idea anyway.

The alternative is to seek open communication. The couple that wrestles issues to the ground wants closeness. If that becomes the style for Adrian, then he can affirm his decision openly—"I am doing this"—once the discussion is over. It will not have to be kept under wraps. It will be known and become the next thing to deal with. Couples who want to deal with things stay together. *Is that what some of us really fear?* What is our real agenda, fearless closeness or fear-based avoidance of it?

In some close relationships, we find ourselves walking on eggshells—that is, fearing being triggered again, feeling anxious about ongoing triggers in our time together. Walking on eggshells is a sign that triggers are happening too often. It may be that one partner, knowing the other's fear or trigger points, uses them to manipulate her. The one who created the eggshell floor is maintaining distance. The one walking is putting up with fear.

Likewise, as we become more familiar with our own triggers, we might invent complex strategies to avoid having them occur. For instance, we might fear someone's wrath or disapproval. We then placate or curry favor lest we upset him or her. Later, we might feel ashamed of ourselves for being timid or obsequious. So then we feel anger at the other because we believe we are being forced into doing what we don't want to do—even though it was always our choice. In fact, the human journey is meant to move from having a parent as a boss who directs our actions to having a partner or friend who loves equality. The more equality in relationships, the fewer the triggers.

Finally, we might use fear as a protective device because we don't know yet whether we can trust a prospective or present partner. The fear then provides a buffer, a boundary that keeps us safe from making a rash decision. This fear-as-reluctance keeps us from jumping into something that is not good for us. We might use anger or ongoing resentment in the same way. They help us keep our distance when our impulsive heart may be foolish enough to move too close to what can sting us.

PRACTICES FOR FREEING OURSELVES
FROM THE GRIP OF FEAR

Even a little progress is complete freedom from fear.

—*Bhagavad Gita*

Fear thrives on convincing us there is no way out, no alternative to the catastrophe that we imagine awaits us, no strategy to free ourselves from the stubborn grip of terror. We are actually in the stubborn grip of myopia, tying ourselves to only one meaning, believing there is only one valid interpretation, imagining only one possible consequence. This is how fear thrives. We fail to see that all thought, especially a fear-based thought, is partial—that a sky of possibilities is hidden behind the one cloud we are fixated on. It is ultimately a restricted imagination that causes our panic. What makes fear so disempowering is our deluded belief that its consequences are inescapable.

The following simple four-step practice can be an empowering resource when we feel ourselves triggered into a fear reaction:

1. *Admit* to yourself and someone you trust that you are afraid. Use that word, not euphemisms like "uncomfortable" or "a bit uneasy."
2. *Allow* yourself to feel your fear fully, with no escape, denial, or distraction.
3. *Act as if* or *Accept with trust*. At this step, we have a twofold choice:

   - *Act as if*: If what we fear is something we can change, we *act as if our fear had no power to drive us to do something or to stop us from doing anything.* This is not acting as pretending but as behaving in a new way. To act in spite of fear is to be courageous. We will never be able to stop ourselves from feeling fear. But we don't have to be bullied by it, either.

- *Accept with trust*: If what we fear is something we can't change, we accept that fact and the uncertainty of the outcome. We *accept* that we don't have control and we *trust* that our inner resources will kick in when the outcome occurs.

Here is a somatic practice for acceptance with trust in ourselves when we feel fear about what might happen: We hold our hand warmly and gently on the part of our body where we feel the anxiety—for example, stomach or throat. We take deep breaths, and with each in-breath we say silently, "Yes to what is and what might be." This is an acceptance of the known fact as well as the as-yet-unknown outcome. With the out-breath we say silently, "I trust myself to handle whatever happens." We repeat this until we calm down, then add one final breath.

Here is an example of combining the Act and Accept steps: Your doctor suggests a medical test for a serious disease, but you are afraid to take the test. Here you "act as if" or "act so that" the fear could not stop you, and you go ahead and take the test. Then you are waiting for the results and you fear what they might be. Here you use the "accept with trust" technique.

4. *Affirm* your own courage in the moment. Any or all of the affirmations in the appendix at the end of this book can help enormously with this affirmation part of the practice. Here you have two goals: asserting your courage and desensitizing yourself from what scares you.

There is no terror . . . in your threats
For I am armed so strong in honesty
That they pass by me as the idle wind.

—Shakespeare, *Julius Caesar*

MINDFULNESS AND LOVING-KINDNESS
FOR FEARLESSNESS

Fear triggers us to cling to what might please us or to run from what might harm us. However, Buddhist teaching—that is, the Dharma—helps us access inner resources that liberate us from those compulsions. For instance, it is natural to us to grab and clutch what appeals to us and to reject and avoid what is not appealing. Attraction and repulsion are frequent trigger reactions for all of us. Buddhism offers a new way of responding—not attaching and not escaping. We do not cling to what is attracting us, nor do we run from what is repulsive to us. We simply notice the shape of what faces us, notice our triggers and instinctive reactions, and then let go of having to choose either option. We hold our experience rather than grip or be gripped by it. For instance, even though our relationship is secure, our ongoing abandonment fear compels us to keep asking our partner for reassurances. In mindfulness, we simply notice our fear and give up checking—unless real evidence of abandonment appears. We do not try to allay our fear by finding an assurance externally. We witness from our prefrontal cortex rather than react from our triggered amygdala. Mindfulness gives us something to do with our agitation. We are no longer at the mercy of triggers because we are witnesses of them. The best next step is to see them with compassion and even amusement.

Sigmund Freud described the equivalent of what we call mindfulness in his "Recommendations for Physicians on the Psycho-Analytic Method of Treatment": "Making no effort to concentrate the attention on anything in particular, and in maintaining with regard to all that one hears, the same measure of calm, quiet attentiveness, of evenly hovering attention." In this mindful style we pay attention to the flow of thoughts and feelings in ourselves. We allow them to pass through us without stopping to examine, judge, or entertain them. When we really are in the moment mindfully it is impossible to keep holding on. Paradoxically, by not reacting we grow in awareness of what things and events are in themselves, before we dressed them up with our projections, desires, fears, add-ons. This is how mindfulness helps us with desensitization: We are no longer so triggered by our cravings and repulsions. We shift from reactions to triggers to pure awareness of what happens out there and in ourselves. Soon the triggers show themselves for what they really are: facts to look at, not self-constructed fictions to grasp onto or escape from.

Fear—and self-doubt—are like the weather, not like house arrest. No matter what the conditions they do not stop us from going out and doing what we have to do that day. Fear is an atmosphere that does not have to be an interference.

As we saw above, Buddhism teaches us to avoid suffering by not attaching to what is transient. Yet, in our loving-kindness practice we can still love ourselves and all beings in the midst of suffering, sometimes even more than when all is well. So why do we put so much energy into avoiding suffering? As long as love is possible in the midst of our pain, suffering is a path to depth, compassion, and redemption.

Love is the antidote to fear. Our full breadth of affection appears when our love comes in closer and goes out farther. We love ourselves and expand our circle of love to include all beings. How do we bring love in closer to ourselves and let it extend out farther to others? Buddhism offers the practice of loving-kindness, also called *metta*—the Pali word for benevolence, well-wishing.

A simple entry technique for the practice of loving-kindness is to picture ourselves in the center of concentric circles. The first and innermost circle, beside or around us, includes those we love personally—for example, family, friends, or partner. Moving out, the next circle is composed of people about whom we feel neutral. The next circle includes people with whom we have difficulty, enemies, opponents. The final, outer circle includes all beings. We beam our love equally to those in each circle, beginning with ourselves—"May I be happy"—and then "May those I love be happy," and so on. We can use this practice daily. We thereby find the "more" that personal love can be—that is, it can be limitless and unconditional. Now we have found the most powerful remedy for fear. It is this universality of love. As an aside, we can notice that our unconscious sometimes does *metta*, shows loving-kindness. An example is having a dream in which we act kindly toward an enemy or are embraced by a lover who left us.

As we engage in the loving-kindness practice that Buddha taught, we also find a sense of connection to our own Buddha nature. We can feel our Buddha nature as a power higher than ego yet ordinary too. When Buddha says, "Be a refuge to yourself," the "yourself" is you just as you are, at your best or worst. Our true refuge is not our fully enlightened nature as all-perfect. It is simply our day-in, day-out being, the one that makes one mistake after another. Thus, our Buddha nature is a refuge, a place to deposit our mistakes and our missed chances at love. Having our Buddha nature as such a repository makes it no longer shameful to be inadequate, erroneous, or adrift. We recall also that the word "refuge" means "fly back"—so appropriate to our coming home to who we are, the home that turns out to be the capacious palace of enlightenment.

Our minds are not equipped to know the infinite, but we touch into it when we put ego aside, sit in the silence of our true nature, and show unconditional loving-kindness. In fact, Buddha nature is described as loving-kindness as well as compassion, joy, and equanimity—all spiritual inner resources. When we trust the true nature of all that is, Buddha nature, and see ourselves as participants in it, we have all those spiritual resources to draw on. Every resource any human ever had is accessible, the basis of hope, the foundation of self-trust.

People of faith can turn to God, who is also described as a Oneness around us and inside us. We see this inner divinity described in a letter by Benjamin Franklin in 1788: "We have a Constitution and I hope future generations will transform its thoughts and make for themselves a place where Life can experiment with its truthfulness and human beings can discover their *divinity in their humanity.*" Thus, we go to the divine—not above, but as an inner resource.

The following outline provides a summary of the three feelings we have explored in these three chapters on sadness, anger, and fear with descriptions of how they show themselves in the experience of triggering.

WHEN WE ARE TRIGGERED BY:	WE MIGHT REACT BY FEELING:	OUR RESOURCES ARE:
Loss	Sadness	Grieving and letting go
Injustice or frustration	Anger	Practices of healthy anger rather than abuse
Threat or danger	Fear	Feeling our fear while not being driven or stopped by it, and affirming our courage to handle it

SEVEN

RELATIONSHIP TRIGGERS AND RESOURCES

Partners in romantic relationships naturally trigger one another. This follows from the fact that our choice of a partner has so much to do with transference from our past. We often unconsciously choose a partner who reminds us of the parent with whom we have unfinished emotional business, hoping to work out as adults what we could not work out in childhood. We are often triggered by something a partner says or does because it has resurrected a pattern of abuse, distress, or unfinished emotional concerns from our past. We might say that the part has triggered the whole. That explains why our reaction is overblown. It also shows us the real issue a trigger points to: the need for our own work on our own past. When we do this work, we still speak up about what triggered us in our relationship. What changes is that we do it in a matter-of-fact way. We are reporting an impact, not heaping blame and pouring out vitriol, not triggering our partner but communicating with her; this is an act of love.

We don't have to fall back on using a trigger finger in our relationships; we can move away from being at the mercy of triggers. An essential feature of healthy communication is to know one another's triggers. We tell one another from the very beginning of the relationship what our triggers are. Then our partner can avoid going there, or he or she can help us work on the issues from our own past that activate our trigger reactions.

Once we know each other's triggers we agree not to pull them. This builds trust: "I can be vulnerable by telling you my trigger points, what my buttons are, and you will not use that information to push my buttons." To know what triggers the other and to use that information to manipulate or frustrate him or her is the style of a toxic partnership, not the style of a loving one.

We can distinguish two kinds of triggers that appear especially in relationships. The first trigger is one that a partner pulls purposely to annoy or hurt the other, with a malicious or mean intent. In this instance, the triggering partner may later feel appropriate guilt and can make amends. The second kind of trigger is one that is simply a given of life, a possibility that is implicit in any relationship. For instance, one partner announces her desire to break up. The other partner is triggered, but a breakup is something that can happen to anyone; it can be an ending with no intent to hurt. The partner who is leaving needs to feel no guilt, only grief and compassion.

When we are triggered, we tell our partner that it is happening and where it comes from, and we can ask for help getting ourselves back on the matter-of-fact track and off the trigger mode. That kind of communication is another way to show healthy vulnerability and build trust. Such vulnerability is not self-victimization, but courage.

We usually treat triggers entirely as *interactions*: "You triggered me, and you are to blame." We can instead look for our *inner reactions*: What happened in us during the interaction? The partner who triggers us is then a more minor player in our drama. Blaming is always an avoidance of our own work, whether that work involves looking into ourselves or making a decision about where to go from here. Blaming means that the ball is never in our court, which is a no-win game.

A trigger is subjective most of the time. When one partner is triggered, the other cannot discount the impact of what he said or did simply by protesting "I did not mean it that way." Our personal list of trigger points calls for respect from our partner because they are real for us—but that respect works in reverse, as well. If our partner tells us she is triggered by what we said or did, we cannot reply, "That doesn't make sense. That should not have triggered you!" In a respectful relationship, any trigger reported by a partner should evoke attention and respect. It does not have to be logical to us. Indeed, all of us, anyone, can feel anxiety sometimes out of nowhere, for no logical reason. Our compassion grows when we see that triggers work the same way.

On the other side, the partner who was triggered may become strident and repetitive about her pain when it is dismissed as illogical. Conflict persists in relationships from such frustrating interactions. Hearing and being heard go a long way toward healing. So can an "Ouch!" and an "Oops!"

Partners can foster an attitude of taking care of one another's triggers whenever possible: For instance, one partner is triggered by dishes left in the sink, so the other makes sure to wash them consistently. One partner is triggered by going to the dentist, so the other partner goes to the appointment with her.

When a partner triggers us we can override our reaction and go directly to what she is saying, feeling, needing. We put aside the personal hurt or defense the trigger would normally evoke in us. For example, say a partner says something critical. We are triggered because our mother criticized us in the same way. Instead of going with the triggered reflex of anger, we swat away that old pterodactyl and focus on our partner, without complaint or comeback. Instead we become curious: *We pause and direct our attention to what our partner is really saying, needing, feeling.* Eventually, criticism from a partner may come through without a mother association. A statement then no longer triggers—it only informs us of where our partner is coming from. Soon we come back to what we both want to say, what we both need, what we both feel. Then, later, when we are alone, we can look at whatever personal work, especially childhood-related, we ourselves need to focus on.

Sometimes a thing that was endearing and charming in a partner's manner or actions in the romance phase may, in the conflict stage, become quite obnoxious and triggering. And sometimes partners continually trigger each other with no letup and with no commitment to changing that style; they seem invested in only blaming one another. There is then, sadly, very little hope for the relationship to survive. Healthy relationships can only thrive when partners acknowledge and work on their triggers in a no-fault zone.

A partner who is triggered may come back with criticism, which then triggers the other. The healthy alternative is giving constructive feedback—such feedback is less likely to be triggering. The stress level caused by a trigger will lessen exponentially when what the other person does or says no longer hits us so hard. This lightening up of an impact is ultimately the goal in working on triggers. As we gain equanimity, we take what a partner, or anyone, says or does more in stride. We find it easier to make allowances; we no longer become so ego-affronted. When the arrow of upset does not penetrate so deeply, we are more apt to *witness* our relationship with patience—and even curiosity. We spend less time causing fires and putting them out, and more time on understanding one another. In this way, the even-keel relationship with its close co-captains on the ship *Commitment* is more likely to find clear sailing.

Some triggers are based on an image of or belief about a partner or friend implanted in us by another person. As a mindfulness practice, we can eschew such secondhand triggering, especially in familial and intimate relationships. We can commit ourselves to relate to people in our life based on our own daily experience, not on gossip about them by others. We decide not to allow others' judgments or impressions to contaminate our relationships. We ask for the same respect toward us: "You are who you are to me only because of how I experience you. I ask that I be who I am to you based only on how you experience me." How others are triggered can't recruit us to abandon one another—though it may open a sincere dialogue about what we have been told.

Sometimes the problem is *not* being triggered to action when it is appropriate! In all my now fifty years of being a psychotherapist the single most common problem I have encountered in clients has been staying too long in a relationship, situation, job, or belief system that does not work—that is unfulfilling or even painful. We are not really staying; we are idling, not moving and wasting resources at the same time. We blunt the trigger that might lead us to change something for the better or to abandon ship. We should not feel too ashamed to undertake change when it is called for. After all, this passage in the Declaration of Independence, written in 1776, makes that very case: "All experience has shown that mankind are more disposed to suffer, while evils are sufferable, than to right themselves by abolishing the forms to which they are accustomed. But . . . it is their right, it is their duty, to throw off such government, and to provide new guards for their future security." No one will make our changes for us. It will take "independence," the resource in all of us, so often inactivated or, sadly, even feared. Finally, we can gently remind ourselves that trying to hold on to a relationship—or anything—beyond its expiration date does not align with the Buddha's teaching on impermanence.

TRUE COMPANIONS

We are social beings, so it is appropriate and praiseworthy that we enlist others to come through for us when we are in need. People share their resources with us. We then discover our own similar resources. We might say *we gain from others' strength and then can find it in ourselves.* For instance, when someone stands up for us, she is showing us her assertiveness and helping us find our own voice too. When someone assists us in facing something, he is showing us how to remain present to ourselves. Such mutual support is an essential feature of friendship and intimacy. All relationships that work, intimate or otherwise, reveal and build resources. The alternative is a sense of isolation and we feel it like a punch in the stomach. The stuffing being knocked out of us is a metaphor for our store of resources being ransacked. Companionship through thick and thin, accompaniment through storm and stress—this is our vital need when the going gets rough. These are the resources a healthy relationship offers.

"She's the one" does not necessarily forecast "We can be together successfully." Sometimes the fact that we still love someone is used to hold us back from moving on with our own life when the other is no longer a true companion. When someone says, "My needs are not fulfilled here but I love him and therefore I will stay and endure," love has become an excuse for an interrupted journey. The healthy adult choice in any relationship is to form connection *and* experience self-actualization—not one at the cost of the other. We seek to maintain the connection while simultaneously increasing an appropriate sense of our own autonomy. That is the advantage of the inner resource of self-confidence to a relationship.

It is paradoxical that we keep *trying to get* our needs met from those who failed us before and fail us now. We might keep trying to change reality when we are afraid of facing it. The more empowering approach is to *give up trying* to get our needs met from those who failed and fail us. Instead, we mourn for what isn't there to be had, and we move on: We accept our own reality without resentment toward or censure of anyone else.

The hope for change in the other and the attempt to get our needs met when the evidence is against it happening are ways of avoiding our grief about the fact of what has been lost or missing, the fact of refusals to our requests for closeness.

An enduring sense of nonfulfillment shows us we have hung around too long in a ghost town. If we really want intimacy, will we find it from loitering longer in the dry saloon? What if we are simply taking turns spinning the roulette wheel? We come to know our authentic agenda in a relationship by asking searching questions of ourselves and one another, without demand or blame:

- Do we want assurance of connection but not really want to do what it takes to establish commitment or communion?
- Have we been programming our choices and responses for more closeness or more distance?
- Have we let go of our attachment to being right?
- Do we still demand that the other should change with the idea that "and then all will be OK"?
- Do we keep one another in an uncertain state so that we, or one of us, can be justified in not being in the relationship in a fully committed way?
- When ruptures occur, do we immediately move toward repair or do we resist it?
- When our partner upsets us, do we disconnect or do we simply take a time-out and then come back to address the issue?
- Can we both report thirty consecutive days of friction-free happiness? (It is not safe to discuss marriage or commitment until at least that amount of time elapses. And it is understandable to consider an end to the relationship when a stretch of happiness has not happened for longer than we can remember.)
- Have we settled for mediocrity in our relationship because life together has become so *comfortable*? Or are we earnestly working together to make it *as good as the best it ever was?*
- Is drama the real goal in the relationship rather than lying down together in green pastures to restore our souls?
- How clear, or even appealing, is Mom or Dad's picture in the locket of our relationship?
- How are we giving and receiving the components of love, the five *A*s, to one another?

In a healthy relationship, the five As happen most of the time in a good enough way. We don't expect constant attunement to our needs by our partner, only moments of it. We know it is enough when the last instance was so recent that we can remember it. Misattunements are to be expected in any relationship. They happened to us in infancy when our parents missed our bids for attention to our needs. Yet, very early on we learned to recover from misattunements. That recovery is the origin of self-soothing, an inner resource now.

Attunement is responding to a need or mirroring a feeling with attention, acceptance, appreciation, affection, allowing. We attune to others' needs and we can also attune to our own. The five As are our inner resources, reliable and enduring. With a loving focus both on ourselves and others we begin to notice our own anxieties diminish.

Finally, we can apply the five As to our *practice* of remaining mindfully present: We bring to the here and now an *attentiveness* to what it is in itself, an *acceptance* of it as it is, an *appreciation* for the opportunities to practice—the graces—that it offers, an *affectionate* holding of it, a full *allowing* of it to open in its own way— and we make allowances for our repeated failures. This is how we mirror the moment with self-compassion and thereby access its richest resources. What arises next is a calm trust in our ability to handle any old trigger.

Tempests never reach into that serenest heaven within where pure and perfect love resides.

—François Fénelon, Jeanne Guyon, and Miguel de Molinos,
A Guide to True Peace

WHEN OUR FEELINGS ARE HURT

A major trigger for all of us is having our feelings hurt either in an intimate relationship or in any interaction. When someone offends us or crosses our boundaries, we have a resource in the recommendations of mental health: Internally, we grieve the event and let it go in accord with our inner timing. With respect to the other person, we express our feelings. We report the impact of his triggering behavior on us using our mindful "Ouch!" In a trustworthy relationship our "Ouch!" will be followed by a sincere "Oops!" from the other. In a healthy relationship, *impact matters.* Our "Ouch!" is taken seriously by our partner. This means that we do not try to talk her out of it but really hear it. Even if what we are doing seems harmless in our perspective, we are willing to change our behavior for the sake of the other's well-being: "How this lands on you matters so much that I am glad to let it go so you don't have to suffer." This is caring respect, not codependency.

We are also deeply triggered when someone hates us. Let's look at three ways of responding to hurt feelings or to hate. The first type of response is primitive, from our cave-people origins. It is aggressive, retaliatory. The second is civilized. It is based on a "Golden Rule" commitment to do no harm. The third flows from mature spiritual consciousness. It is an expression of universal and unconditional love. We can respond to someone who hates or hurts us in any one of these three ways. Let's use the example of being snubbed:

1. If someone snubs us, we can snub him back the next time we see him. This is the primitive style of retaliation: "Do as you have been done by."
2. We do not snub him back since we choose to act nonviolently no matter how others behave toward us.
3. In spiritual awareness, we are moved to choose an over-the-top response. We actually do good to the one who has snubbed us, either directly or in our loving-kindness aspirations or prayers for him.

The following outline is a summary of the three choices available to us when people hurt our feelings or hate us. Notice that the three options of response allow us to reset our trigger reactions. We do not have to react from the first one. Now we have two more options in how we can respond.

PRIMITIVE REACTION FROM OUR REPTILIAN BRAIN	COMMITMENT TO "DO NO HARM"	EXPRESSION OF UNCONDITIONAL LOVING-KINDNESS
We hurt or hate back.	We do not hurt or hate back.	We do not hurt or hate back. We go one step further and do good to those who hurt or hate us. This may simply mean having no ill will toward them while wishing them the best, without further contact. In all this we hold an intention to forgive.
We become aggressive, actively or passively. We retaliate to "right the wrong" (in accord with the street-rules style).	We act in accord with ethical principles and a commitment to nonviolence.	We act in accord with the Sermon on the Mount and/or the Buddhist practice of loving-kindness. This includes the possibility that we might even "*love* our enemies."
Adrenaline/ testosterone-driven ego-saving reaction	Oxytocin/heart- motivated sense of respect for all people	Oxytocin/heart-oneness
Heartless	Heart-opening	Heart-expanding
Ego-based—that is, fear-based	Humanism-based	Love-based
"I alone am important!"	"You are important too!"	"We are deeply linked!"
Win-lose	Win-win by two separate individuals	Win-win by two connected individuals
This is giving in to our dark side.	This takes ethical consciousness and ongoing practice.	This takes an openness to grace and a commitment to ongoing practice.

We are like the guys in the *Godfather* movies.	We are like Mister Rogers or Atticus Finch.	We are Christ or Buddha in the world of today.
We hear an avenger's voice: "Do it too."	We hear a mediator's voice: "Don't do it."	We hear Michelle Obama: "When they go low, we go high."
We enjoy the sweetness of revenge, gratify our ego, and are glad we can look good in the eyes of our gang.	We grow in self-respect because we are remaining true to our standards of kindness and evolved consciousness.	We love ourselves and all beings more; we move toward enlightenment/transformation—and we want that for everyone.

Note that the far-right column is counterintuitive. In these responses, we are acting from our higher self, not from our ego. We are awakened by grace in the form of a conversion from selfishness to selflessness, a surrendering of ego-centeredness to love-centeredness. That surrender is not a loss. It is a heart-opening. It is a response to our inborn impulse toward connection, what shows us that in our deepest identity we are love. Thus, our loving-kindness toward all beings is a *self-expression*.

Indeed, our connection to others, our care about them, flows from an awakening to our true nature. This happens as a grace, an enlightened moment, not caused by effort or merited by actions. Awakening is a free gift from the universe, higher power, God, Source, Buddha. Our ego does not motivate us to give generously to others; it is out for itself. Nor can we make ourselves awaken. It comes as a grace given to us. We see this in the twelfth step of the Alcoholics Anonymous program: "Having had a spiritual awakening [by grace] . . . we tried to carry [effort] this message to alcoholics." Notice here that grace is meant to move us toward renewed effort, ongoing action, and enduring commitment to the fellowship of humanity.

As a practice, we can meditate on these heartful recommendations from a variety of traditions. Each proposes a behavior that enacts connectedness, the essence of loving-kindness. Hate, by contrast, enacts separation, the violation of human communion, and it is the cause of our suffering. Love reverses that curse:

> May those whose hell it is to hate and hurt be turned into lovers bringing flowers.
>
> —Shantideva, *The Way of the Boddhisattva*

> Love one another in your hearts, and if anyone offend you, speak with him in peace and banish the venom of hatred, and do not let the revenge abide in your heart.
>
> —*Testaments of the Twelve Patriarchs,* 107 BCE

> Love your enemies, do good to those who hate you, bless those who curse you, pray for those who mistreat you.
>
> —Luke 6:27–28

> Sooner or later all the people of the world will have to discover a way to live together in peace. . . . If this is to be achieved, we must evolve for all human conflict a method which rejects revenge, aggression, and retaliation. The foundation of such a method is love.
>
> —Martin Luther King Jr., in his speech accepting the 1964 Nobel Peace Prize

DIFFICULT PATTERNS IN RELATIONSHIPS

Why do we keep repeating the very patterns that will sabotage our relationships? Patterns take the form of one partner's reaction to a triggering behavior followed by mutually triggering arguments. But there is another dimension, deeper than action-reaction. We can unearth at least three levels in a relationship pattern:

1. The Triggering Event: What Happened

The first level of a relationship pattern is the triggering event. The broken agreement or unacceptable behavior or event that keeps happening is the narrative, the story: "You do this and I get triggered." The partner either denies it happened that way or says there is a justifiable explanation. Now each partner may have—and cling to—a different narrative. That brings the conflict up to a second level:

2. The Drama: Arguing about What Happened

At the second level, an argument, a dramatic flare-up ensues. Each partner is intent on proving that his or her own actions and reactions are justified. This turns into continual back-and-forth triggering. There is no processing of feelings, only each partner maintaining their position based on individual interpretations, projections, assumptions about what happened. Neither partner may guess that there is another motivation at work:

3. The Unconscious Agenda behind It All

The dimension of the third level—the unconscious agenda behind it all—is the most cunning and elusive, since it is outside our awareness. Usually, we need help in finding out what we are really up to. We are unconsciously motivated into an intimacy-defeating pattern. Yet, all the while, we are focusing only on the first two levels, both triggering, so both confounding. The two conscious levels of dispute and drama have to be traced to their hidden agenda, the deeper truth that activated them. Only then can we break out of the pattern.

Agendas are based on motives. The following list offers examples of agenda-motivations that can sabotage a relationship. One or more of these might be up and running in the midst of our conflicts:

- This relationship was a mistake to begin with and I am doing something that will spring me out of it.
- I can't leave this relationship on my own; I want to force her to make me go.

- It is dangerous to be in any relationship with both feet in, so I can't ever be fully committed.
- I am actively and passively getting back at him—or a parent or former partner—for an old hurt.
- I am maintaining my sense of entitlement. I believe I have a right to full agency, control, and decision-making. Thus, I can reject collaboration.
- I am in this relationship to gratify my own ego, not to let go of my ego to fulfill the relationship.
- I am addicted to adrenaline, so keeping things at fever-pitch and unresolved gives me the fix I came here for. I get antsy when there is too much smooth sailing. Something in me has to cause shipwreck or at least a perfect storm.
- I only feel good when I do what leads my partner to feel upset or crazy.
- I want to prove my worst fear, perhaps based on an abandonment experience in the past: *He won't be there for me when I am really in need* or *I don't matter enough for him to be loyal to me for the long haul.* This makes me not trust him. I then have to put energy into a contingency plan, which can take the form of complaint, blame, or keeping an eye out for a new partner.
- I have to train her to be like my mother or father so I can re-experience a positive or negative pattern from childhood.
- I fear and avoid intimacy at all costs.

In each of these, we set things up so that we will find *evidence* that our agenda is legitimate. What a way to stay stuck: "I get you to do what proves me right and what assures us no progress." Any progress toward more closeness is highly dangerous when one's safety seems possible only by distancing—the common theme in all the examples above.

If a man's agenda is avoiding being engulfed by his partner, he now feels justified in his agenda. The other partner may take the distancing as an abandonment, replicating what her father did. Her agenda may be to prove that all men will leave her. The confirmation of an agenda will be considerably more satisfying than conflict-resolution and an effective relationship.

What can help us toward healing is to uncover our agenda, admit our motivations, and design a new positive agenda: I am in this to show the five As and ask for them, to behave lovingly, to act collaboratively, to address, process, and resolve conflicts as they arise, to ask for what I need directly.

This final suggestion about directness gives us our best chance at casting light on our secret agenda. We ask what our agenda is meant to make happen. Or, even more telling, we can ask what keeps happening in the relationship when we have conflicts. *Where we wind up over and over is the most useful clue to the true agenda of each partner.* For instance, if what we end up in again and again is distance, that may be our agenda. But wait! Distance as space helps us grow; it does not have to mean abandonment. Nor does closeness have to mean engulfment. We can ask for healthy distance directly rather than by defaulting to what happens when our agenda is secret: which is that we try to achieve distance in roundabout ways. In healthy relating, when we do ask for distance, we add a word about returning to our connection: "I need some time to myself now and I will be back by seven for dinner." We are asking for what we need and giving assurance that our request does not indicate abandonment. Now we don't have to go through so many gyrations to fulfill the secret agenda that stresses us and confuses or hurts our partner—and us too.

Finally, every hidden agenda is fueled by fear. To ask ourselves what we are most afraid of is a useful open sesame into our hidden agendas. Look again at the bulleted list above. Every entry, without exception, holds a fear—for some of us, even a terror. The fears are not new. They are familiar, lodged in us for decades. We look back and realize how these are the exact fears that designed so many of our choices—and later our regrets. In the book of Genesis, when

God questions Adam's secrecy, Adam explains, "I was afraid, so I hid myself." Indeed, there is a direct connection between what we fear and what we keep hidden. Both sabotage our chances at the serene intimacy that can bring us happiness. That option thrives on fearless openness, the openness that leads a partner to trust us. So we gain all the way around.

STATES OF THE UNION

Here are examples of some of the many sectors of a marriage or of a seriously committed relationship: love, friendliness, loyalty, candid communication, sharing of feelings, fulfillment of financial obligations, cohabitation, co-parenting, sexual connection, sharing of similar interests, bilateral decision-making, collaboration in practical matters. All these elements flourish as a unity only when both partners are still on board in activating them. However, sometimes one partner or both are no longer committed to tending to all the domains of a marital union. For instance, one partner may be acting irresponsibly regarding the budget. The other partner then takes over that sector. The partners are now not partnered financially. In effect, they are no longer "married" in that subdivision of their bond. This will naturally trigger resentment in the partner who feels obliged to take over. The same imbalance can happen in the realm of child-rearing as another example.

When just about all areas of the bond have collapsed, except cohabitation and financial contribution, the partners have, in effect, become roommates. Their full commitment is no longer operational. When one or both spouses are no longer in the relationship with both feet, they are no longer fully married. The "partners" still have a marriage certificate, but it has been rendered inactive. Usually, their annulment is known to both of them but not talked about. This is an instance in which a trigger is needed to signal a need for a change, but no trigger is firing it up.

It would be of great advantage to make the implicit bargain explicit: "Let's admit that a diminished commitment is all that is left of our relationship. Do we want to keep it this way or re-enfranchise a full marriage? Some states have seceded from our union. Do we want to bring them back in without triggering a civil war?"

Let's consider another dilemma that may arise. If there is no sex, or intention of having it happen, is a partner justified in finding that component elsewhere? Can he or she say: "We are now divorced at the sexual level, so I believe that either of us is free to devise a new sexual plan. The alternative of no sex with another person for the rest of my life is not acceptable." This is a topic that calls for openness and for therapy if partners are to explore what is happening and then decide what comes next. They may find that a breakdown in one or some areas of a commitment is the equivalent of a breakup. They may also choose to restore the missing links.

At the same time, a relationship or marriage can be designed entirely by the adult participants. Thus, a marriage in which there is no sex or in which there is an unequal financial arrangement can be indeed legitimate if both partners are truly satisfied with it. A sexless relationship may have longevity, but the partners might still wonder if they are finding the full measure of growth, challenge, and happiness a partnership can provide. Wise people open a long conversation when they decide to omit something so important to the fulfillment of universal human longings.

DANGER IN THE ELECTRONICS SECTOR?

Screens are often between us today. We wonder how the focus on electronic gadgetry, especially in young people, is impacting the possibility of true connection. Does it obstruct or foster relating?

In the pre-electronic age, we grew up interfacing with others only by direct contact. We could understand how others felt by reading their feelings, faces, words, gestures. In a world of online meetings, however, our emotional range becomes stunted. So many of us are now caught up in the speed style of texting, compulsive checking for messages, calling one another to check on whereabouts, obsessive Facebook reporting of minor daily issues. All this seems to increase communication, but it actually inhibits social contact and the gaining of skills for human connection. The electronic world can in fact ultimately make isolation rewarding. Human love is changing, not because our capacity for love is lessening but because the authentic ways of getting to it can now take a backseat to virtual connections. We notice, for instance, our preference for texting rather than talking by phone, let alone meeting up.

The immediacy of the search-engine click-to-an-answer becomes a style that can make taking time to find solutions intolerable. In this regard, we are shortening our attention span. We receive reinforcement from making quick moves toward whatever is next, not from sustained attention. No wonder we see such an increase in attention deficit disorder in our population. Sustained attention is the first of the five *As*, the components of intimacy. Our addiction to the virtual world has to have an effect on how we show intimate love. How is it possible for those who cannot abide taking time to work something out be candidates for time-taking relationships and conflict resolution? How can those who have not learned to pay attention for very long listen carefully to another person? How can someone whose every spare moment has to be filled with stimulation be able to handle the many flatline hours and longueurs that inevitably punctuate a life together?

Some young people don't like reading a novel because exciting things don't happen on every page and it takes too long to get to the denouement. But our brain thrives on a sequence of stimulation and then enough downtime for processing and synthesizing what we have read or learned. The loss of this simmering phase, and the time it requires, debits from our skill at processing experiences and problems, especially in relationships. Since simmering is crucial to freeing ourselves from triggers, this presents an obstacle to accessing inner resources.

Shakespeare writes in *Twelfth Night*:

O time, thou must untangle this, not I.
It is too hard a knot for me to untie.

But we no longer have hard knots or the need for time to untie them because the internet has ready answers to all our conundrums, no matter how complex. To doubt complexity because now everything is so simple and at our fingertips is to doubt the full potential of human relationships with all their dead-ends and disappointing chimeras. We do not gain the skills of waiting and pausing, of facing our own demons one-by-one *at their pace*, of slowly reconstituting ourselves after crises. Those struggles are the building blocks of inner resources and meaningful relationships.

In my childhood in the fifties we saw a movie on a Saturday afternoon and then played the parts of the actors with our friends. We wanted to emulate the heroes. That night, we pictured what happened in the film in our imagination as we went to sleep. Those are all ways the psyche evolves. It does not fare well when we see one film after another with no time to contemplate their meaning, live with their themes, relate them to our own story, find the metaphor for our own life in them.

All the skills required to be human and to be intimate seem to be at stake, and only time will tell if we have something to worry about here or if it will all work itself out satisfactorily.

We have developed technologies that make change possible. We can see this advance as a metaphor for our personal work: We can perhaps now develop technologies of love so that the world will change because of our new collective ways of connecting. It takes cooperation and collaboration, forms of caring. Globalization is connection but not yet caring connection, the essence of love. Do we have the power of gods because we need to conquer and command or because we were meant to be what we say God is: love?

The day will come when, after harnessing space, the winds, the tides, and gravitation, we shall harness for God the energies of love. And on that day, for the second time in the history of the world, we shall have discovered fire.

—Pierre Teilhard de Chardin, *Toward the Future*

PRACTICES THAT INCREASE OUR RELATIONSHIP RESOURCES

Certain practices can increase the resources that strengthen our relationships and reduce the impact of our triggers and reactions, as in the following examples.

Who Picks a Partner?

With healthy inner resources we are attracted to healthy people. When the picker is the part of us that wants to complete the past, we might not be so discerning in our choice. A person who was brought up by a mother who continually hurt or betrayed him might now feel the need to continue to be a victim of a woman's dishonesty. It is counterintuitive but often the case. Remember that we look for a repeat of the past—not an alternative to it—when we have not worked our history out. In other words, we prefer repetition to innovation—a self-defeating choice indeed.

Our need from childhood to make Mommy come through this time diminishes our powers of intelligent assessment. Unmet needs make us continuously scan our world to look for the one who can fulfill them, but mistakenly. We hook up with a partner who betrays us over and over. The possibility of finding out he is not trustworthy is more familiar and therefore in some ways more satisfying to the wounded child within. She seeks repeat of the past, not freedom from it. This is how the psyche puts first things first: it does the personal work of clearing up the past, and only then finds a healthy alternative to it. With inner resources, however, we can make choices based on what works rather than what echoes.

On a humorous note, if, impossibly, we had ever actually completed all the work necessary to clear up our unfinished business from childhood, then who would attract us?

Boundaries

By the age of three months babies routinely employ a "stimulus barrier" to protect themselves from too much input. For instance, if an adult is trying to arouse their interest and they are tired, babies simply close their eyes and doze or turn away. We can use similar techniques but with words: "I need some alone time now, so let's talk later." This is an alternative to running away or angrily turning on the other. In addition, we learn we can survive when we are triggered by the fact that a partner is getting too close for comfort. We can ask for space without offending, triggering, our partner.

Two-Way Mindfulness

In mindfulness practice we are nonjudgmental witnesses of our here and now experience. In such personal practice we are mindful *of*. But wait! In an intimate relationship we can also be mindful *toward*. Partners can practice being present to one another in a nonjudging, nondemanding, noncontrolling way. We will definitely feel the power of this interactive style of mindfulness. It will be especially meaningful when one of us is going through a hard time. We will be comforted in our distress when our partner sits with us in serene mindful attentiveness. Such *real presence* endows us with a secure sense of being loved and respected, of being cared about and understood. It is the equivalent of physical holding.

This two-way experience of mindfulness is crucial in how we reduce what we might call "inter-triggering" in our relationships. We are less likely to trigger one another when we feel held in our experience rather than shamed, criticized, or blamed for it. Indeed, two-way mindfulness in any interaction, whether at home or work, is a royal road to connectedness and mutual respect.

Loving Ourselves and Being Loved

Feeling loved is a positive trigger; feeling unloved is a negative one. Real love can't be earned, only given freely. That is what we sound like when we love ourselves; we are not redesigning ourselves to please others, only opening to others just as we are: "I will just be who I am and see who responds with love." Shakespeare presents a helpful practice in *Measure for Measure*, expressing the great affirmation against self-deception: "Now I will unmask."

We might also be aware that someone looking at us with love activates our love for ourselves: "I must be very lovable if she loves me so much." This is how love from others increases our inner resources.

Finally, we love ourselves when we act lovingly toward all people. The loving-kindness cycle moves from self to all beings. By loving all we feel ourselves included in the love that is everywhere.

May I show all the love I have,
In any way I can, wherever I may be,
Today and everyday,
To everyone—including me—
Since love is what we are
And why we're here.
Now nothing matters to me more
Or gives me greater joy.
May all our world become
One Sacred Heart of love.

Letting Go of Having to Win

When our competitive ego is triggered, we will be driven by the need to be right—a form of stress and pain. But true safety in an intimate relationship can't happen when someone has to be right. It comes from freeing ourselves from the ego-fear of not being in control. Then both partners find themselves safely and securely in an environment that is generous and no-fault. That environment is more likely to happen when we are flexible. This does not mean we give up our convictions in order to purchase safety. It does mean that we have found the knack of maintaining our beliefs and boundaries without forcing others to bow to our superiority, an action that will certainly push their buttons. Instead, we are open to others' views. We look for ways to find common ground rather than to be on top.

Need without Judgment

It is so hard to express a need without it coming across as a judgment, a censure of the other: "I need more affection" seems to equal "You are not giving affection to me enough." So the partner reacts by going on the defensive, feeling attacked, judged as inadequate. We can more appropriately express emotional needs this way: "You are good at giving affection and it makes me want more of it. How about doing it together now?" That statement does not pull a trigger.

We can learn to express any need without accusing the other of inadequacy. For instance, we can say, "I need the coriander for this dish," and our partner hands it to us, a clear transaction. But when we say, "I needed coriander and I asked you to get it on your way home, but you just don't listen to me," that is judgment.

Our discussion of the presence of others in this book has been described as an accompaniment and a showing of the five As. Alternatively, our presence with others comes through when we are vulnerable, especially in expressing our needs and wounds. We are present in a relationship when we declare our longings, show the holes in our hearts, open our soul with all its stammering cries for help and caring. We will feel awkward sharing our needs, but only because we have not practiced enough. We feel vulnerable because the other might say no or might promise and not follow through. But our courage in finally and fully telling someone who we are trumps all that. Courage emboldens us so that vulnerability becomes landscape, not earthquake. That landscape is, wonderfully,

> the dreamt land
> Toward which all hungers leap, all pleasures pass.
> —Richard Wilbur, "A Baroque Wall-Fountain in Villa Sciarra"

The Good-Natured Shrug

Once we know the personality of a partner, friend, or family member, we come to expect certain behaviors and attitudes. Yet some of these traits still trigger us, and we react with what leads to an argument. We find a stress-reducing resource, however, when we shrug off what they say or do rather than make it a bone of contention. We take their words and behaviors in stride, no longer getting into an argument, no longer making any attempts to fix, change, or control them or show how wrong they are. This is not giving up on them or not listening. It is finally respecting who they are, accepting the givens of their personality. We don't shrug off abuse—that, we confront. We do shrug off what others do that triggers us. Fewer triggers mean more intimacy. *Is this what we are fleeing?*

Personal Work

Intimacy is built on doing the personal work on ourselves that makes us more open and present. Personal work promotes and enhances connection. Doing our personal work is not only a way to make life easier in a relationship. It is also a way of showing love for someone because we do what it takes for intimacy to thrive. Our work shows results like these: We are dealing with the wounds of childhood so we don't transfer them onto our partner. We are acting assertively but not aggressively. We are communicating directly, not passively. We are handling conflicts by addressing, processing, and resolving them each time they arise. We are dealing with daily crises with equanimity rather than taking them out on our partner. Now addressing, processing, and resolving have become not only practices but resources.

On a personal note, I don't fool myself into thinking I have fully achieved equanimity. Indeed, I notice that I have it only when I am not being triggered. For instance, if I have to deal with red tape while traveling, I can be patient rather than triggered, but that is because nothing happened in childhood having to do with red tape. *Is my (or our) ability to have equanimity limited to what has no history?*

EIGHT

SPIRITUAL RESOURCES

Contained in this short Life
Are magical extents.
—Emily Dickinson

The spiritual can be described in one word: "more." This word refers to something transcendent, more than what meets the eye:

- We intuit that there is more to living things than what we see, a deeper reality behind appearances.
- We feel there is more to us than our ego, a larger life in us than personality and personal history.
- We sense that happenings are more than events; they are opportunities for spiritual practice.
- We realize that love is more than feeling good about someone; it is an unconditional and enduring connection and commitment.
- We find more than connection in an intimate partnership; we find communion.
- We move toward more than the goal of self-help in our work on ourselves; we have a sense of service to humanity.
- We act with more than fairness; we show generosity.

Thus, a spiritual consciousness sees:

Nature as more than natural things

Our human identity as more than ego

Time as more than duration

Place as more than location

Our destiny as more than our goals

Our love as able to extend to more people than
our near and dear

We notice that an avaricious person also seeks more. Likewise, an addict seeks more. Their craving does not seem spiritual. Yet they too are yearning for what will take them beyond the limited. They want the limitless. And that is the transcendent after all. The mistake they make is in the addictive object they choose and the dysfunctional strategy they use to possess it. A program—for example, Alcoholics Anonymous—offering contact with a transcendent higher power is therefore a healthy path to a true recovery and spiritual consciousness.

We read this in the preamble to "The Earth Charter": "Human development is primarily about being more, not having more." The "sacred" is the "more" in all that is. That "more" is a spiritual resource. We only see the full reality when we see the sacred in it. When we say yes to the more, we see it in ourselves, others, events, things, places. Everything is sacred. Spiritual life thus means nothing again is ever profane: We have become More, a Yes to the sacred "where all places are."

"Yes" is the only place on earth where all places are.

—Jorge Luis Borges, "The Aleph"

WHEN THE TIME HAS COME

It must have lain hidden in my soul, though I knew nothing of it, and it rose suddenly to my memory when it was needed.

—Fyodor Dostoyevsky, "The Peasant Marey"

There is a gratifyingly positive trigger experience that happens to us every once in a while. It is a sudden "Aha!" or an awakening. It can be a realization, a letting go, a shift, a life-changing moment, a lifting of a weight off our shoulders, a sudden clarity, a feeling of everything coming together to make perfect sense, the moment the penny drops. There will be an event or word or experience that touches it off. It will seem to be a cause of the great awakening. But, actually, it is a launching pad, a catalyst. This awakening is not objective, from outside, but subjective, something happening in us, an example of a spiritual inner resource.

This positive trigger experience is an example of synchronicity, the meaningful coincidence of catalyst and inner timing. Synchronicity is a spiritual experience because it happens as a grace; it is not something we cause. We can only be ready. Some word or event ignites a fire of awareness or of release. Zen stories often tell of a special moment in which someone was suddenly enlightened—for instance, this story of a simple monk in a monastery in Japan. His daily task for years was to sweep the small stones in the garden so that they were evenly spread out. One day while he was sweeping, a single stone hit the wall with a ping. When he heard the ping, he was fully enlightened. The day of awakening had come. The ping was the triggering catalyst. The two events happening at once is the trigger-synchronicity. The catalyst is an instance of grace, the gift dimension of life.

We find another example in the 1959 French film *Hiroshima Mon Amour*, where the main character, deeply depressed, is living in a cellar, immobilized by grief. One day, children are playing with marbles on the ground above her. A marble rolls in through the window onto the floor. She picks it up and holds it in the palm of her hand. When she feels the warmth of the child's hand that had been holding the marble, her depression lifts. The marble did not cause the change; it was a graced moment coinciding with the time for her release.

In one other example, a mother hears again and again that it is not her fault that her daughter is a drug addict. But it makes no impression. Then one day she hears it yet again and she suddenly, physically, feels a weight lifting up off her shoulders. The words were the same but until then the timing had not been right for the click of reception.

What is timing? It is a readiness. It can't be manufactured, hurried, or postponed. There is an inner timing to most interior events. Grief is an example. We have to shed a very specific number of tears before we can let it go.

We notice that life offers us two options: (1) We can make conscious choices or (2) things happen to us beyond our control. In every example of a timing-trigger the catalyst is "things happening," not the conscious result of our manipulations. Sometimes the timing is right for willpower, taking the bull by the horns, as Theseus did with the Minotaur. Sometimes the timing is right for willingness, as when he waited for Ariadne to show him the way out of the labyrinth. Our intention is journey; our strategy takes discerning what is ready to happen.

To discern what fits comes as a grace, the mysterious gift moment from a power beyond our ego. It is as if there is something, we know not what, that is always at work to make us more than we are yet. It is as if the universe knows our timing to the exact moment and is patiently planning its advent. It is as if we are not alone. When I come to trust this, I let go of believing that only that will come to pass that I make happen. I come to trust a power beyond my control. When that same power is an inner resource, we are spiritual. We see this in the Big Book of *Alcoholics Anonymous*:

"With few exceptions our members find that they have tapped an unsuspected inner resource which they presently identify with their own conception of a Power greater than themselves."

This stunningly wise quotation also reminds us that our healing and personal integration are not all about effort. We can trust grace, the gift dimension of life, "an unsuspected inner resource" contributing to how we progress on our journey. In this book, I propose building inner resources to handle triggers. I do not mean to repeat the old public-school belief that it is all up to us: we can "pull ourselves up by our bootstraps," we are "captains of our destiny," we are "the little engine that could." That is a limited and limiting cultural bias. It is based on a rugged individualism that overlooks our central evolutionary inclination: to connect and collaborate on the path to progress. Trusting that our challenge in handling triggers includes the support of others and of grace, we do all we can, *and* we rely on others in our support group. We do all we can, *and* we trust a power beyond our ego in whatever way we construe it. Then we are not alone, the scariest fantasy the mind ever conjured—and the least accurate.

NEUROPLASTICITY AND SPIRITUALITY

The brain is like a factory in which each department works cooperatively with all the others. For instance, the prefrontal cortex helps with thinking, decision-making, planning for the future, setting intention, and regulating thought, feeling, and behavior. The hippocampus processes and encodes our memories. The brain stem controls heart rate, breathing, and other autonomic functions. The communication from department to department happens by electrochemical sharing of information along neural pathways. The neural pathways become ingrained when they are used over and over. Thus, our habits are durable, but our new ways of acting do not lock in as easily. Using the metaphor of a factory, the familiar routine operations are done easily—but new projects take more time for the workers to perform.

Neuroplasticity is the power of the brain to change itself, both structurally and operatively, by way of a new focus and alternative habits. We can, in effect, change our negative—self-defeating, dysfunctional—patterns into positive ones, those that serve our life goals. New linkages can be installed in our brain. Neuroplasticity makes change and development possible. It allows us to reverse ingrained habits that do not serve us. We can create new patterns of thought and behavior that help us adapt more effectively to our varying inner landscapes and our pressuring world.

We can also make spiritual progress through neuroplasticity. By engaging in repeated spiritually focused affirmations and morally aware actions, we can help our brain rewire itself so those affirmations and actions become positive habits—that is, virtues. The new pathways, however, do not appear simply by repeating certain thoughts or actions. We bring a highly alert attentiveness to the process. Meditation as focused attention helps us get there. The brain, however, like the work force in a factory, can be easily distracted. It is up to us to manage it by keeping it on track. Indeed, there is a danger that once a new thought or skill becomes second nature, we are less likely to mine for new possibilities. Change does not occur on autopilot—only habit does. So, second nature, less attentiveness, means fewer chances for laying down new pathways in the brain.

We also now know that an entirely mental experience can make for new neural connections. An athlete picturing herself diving in new ways is changing her brain, and then her body, for new dives. We can mirror ourselves through our imagination. William James in his "Talks to Teachers on Psychology and to Students on Some of Life's Ideals" recommended to them: "Put yourself assiduously in conditions that encourage the new way; make engagements incompatible with the old."

The neuroscientist Andrew Newberg, in *How God Changes Your Brain*, demonstrates through his research that meditation increases blood flow to the anterior cingulate. The anterior cingulate is the part of the brain that links our primitive amygdala with our pre-frontal cortex. This is the region of the brain that holds our ability to show caring, empathy, social consciousness. It likewise fosters intuition and helps us regulate our emotions and our reactions to triggers. Dr. Newberg has shown that meditation can firm and fortify the anterior cingulate and reduce the influence of the primitive amygdala. We are then more likely to act in accord with our spiritual values. Indeed, spirituality is not about how good we feel, how close to the divine, how sublime our thoughts. It is about becoming as loving—as connected—as we were born to be. In Buddhist terms spirituality is a daily focused practice of loving-kindness toward ourselves and all beings. Chögyam Trungpa Rinpoche reminds us in *Smile at Fear*: "The practice of meditation is not so much about the hypothetical attainment of enlightenment. It is about leading a good life." Even more, Newberg states that there is "a coevolution of spirituality and consciousness, engaging circuits that allow us to envision a benevolent, interconnecting relationship between the universe, God, and ourselves."

The limbic system regulates our emotions. What is the connection between stressful dramatic emotions and negative thoughts? The physician Daniel Amen—the author of *Change Your Brain, Change Your Life*—has used the imaging technique known as SPECT (single photon emission computed topography) to show that when the limbic system is in a highly stressed state we automatically see the world through a negative lens. When the limbic area is calm, however, we are more likely to find ourselves in a positive frame of mind—a feeling captured in Psalm 23, which makes a connection between "still waters" and "fear no evil."

PRACTICES THAT INCREASE OUR SPIRITUAL RESOURCES

Accessing Our Inner Goodness

Our most prized spiritual resource is inner goodness. Chögyam Trungpa wrote in *Shambhala: The Sacred Path of the Warrior*:

"Every human being has a basic nature of goodness, which is undiluted and unconfused and contains tremendous gentleness and appreciation." Our basic goodness makes love possible. How ironic that what is the best in us we often cover up, doubt, forget, or fear. In *The Brothers Karamazov* by Fyodor Dostoyevsky, Father Zossima advises adopting a spiritual path—resource—when we meet up with hate or evil: "Always choose gentle love." I have kept those words on my desktop for many years. I see them every day many times. I believe they offer me a sublime spiritual path. But I also fully realize I will need to keep this recommendation right here in front of me all my life. There is a dark side of me that will choose aggression automatically at times, triggered or not. In moments of stress I will forget the advice that means so much to me in calm moments. My practice, my work, my calling is to remember "gentle love" and act on it. I thereby access a moment of inner goodness. And it has to be acceptable to me that I do this only "more and more," as "every time" may never happen.

Richard Rohr, in "The Trap of Perfectionism," wrote, "The real victory for me was when I was able to recognize my profound inner experience of *goodness as the core and foundation of all reality*. . . . It is always a kind of crucifixion and surrender of *the idea of goodness for which I long*—instead of the actual goodness that is given." Thus, we can indeed let go of our restrictive definition of goodness and widen its meaning. It transcends our moral formulations; it is the essence of all reality. Goodness is in everything irrespective of our notions of "good" and "bad." This is a deeply spiritual realization because it takes us from an ego definition based on limitation to the limitless universal.

As a spiritual practice we can stay on the lookout for basic goodness in every person we encounter. One way of doing this is to notice when we are judging someone. We take that as a cue that we need to "look for the good and praise it," as the saying goes. This does not mean trying to find an example of niceness in others. It is more challenging than that. It might mean, for instance, that we look for a tender vulnerability behind a hostile frown. We do this not only for others but also for ourselves. Our sense of goodness can widen and deepen so that we recognize it as the mysterious inner life of us and of all that lives. That is so much bigger—and more intriguing—than the definition of goodness based on our insistent calculations of right and wrong. We access our own and others' inner goodness when all judgments end.

> Out beyond ideas of wrongdoing and right-doing
> there is a field. I'll meet you there.
> When the soul lies down in that grass
> the world is too full to talk about.

> —Rumi, "A Great Wagon"

Tonglen Practice

The Tibetan Buddhist practice called *tonglen* is an imaginative spiritual resource for dealing with suffering. It is also useful in working with triggers. Tonglen can take three directions: (1) It can be a way of dealing with our own negative experiences, (2) it can be a compassion exercise for the pain and distress of those around us, or (3) it can be a caring response to suffering the world over.

In Tibetan, the word *tonglen* means "send out and let in." In this practice we are willing to take in what we would usually run away from. We pass it through our evolved consciousness, our hearts of loving-kindness, and it is transformed into healing power.

The first thing we notice is that tonglen is counterintuitive: We hold, rather than flee, the unpleasant experience that has triggered us. We are breathing it in with our conscious in-breath. Yet, as a next step, we are breathing out a healing energy with our out-breath. This is indeed a brave act, so tonglen is always also an antidote to fear!

When we see suffering in others, or feel for how they are triggered, we use the same practice: we breathe in the pain and send out well-being. We can also extend our concern to all beings who are suffering or in crisis. Now we are going beyond our own trigger-reactiveness into universal caring and compassionate love.

To the degree that we can stay present with our own pain, we can hang in with someone who's provoking us. We come to see pain as something that can transform us, not as something to escape at any cost. . . . We'll find ourselves increasingly more able to be there for others, even in what used to seem like impossible situations.

—Pema Chödrön, *Living Beautifully with Uncertainty and Change*

Moving from Superstition to Reality

We can mature into the adult style of understanding reality rather than engaging in wishful thinking and fantasy. We can find new meanings in these common superstitions of the New Age movement:

Everything will work out for the best.
We change that to:
Everything will work out as it does and we will have the opportunity to look for the best in it or make the best of it.

Everything happens for a reason.
We change that to:
Anything can happen and we have the inner resources to find in it a reason for hope.

What goes around comes around.
We change that to:
May what goes around come around in a way that helps us all grow.

God never gives us more than we can bear.
We change that to:

Some traumatic events can crush us but now we have state-of-the-art ways of finding the help we need.

There are no coincidences.
We can change that to:
There are ordinary coincidences based on randomness and there are meaningful coincidences in which the spiritual world breaks into our daily experience.

It all depends on me.
We can change that to:
Grace is everywhere.

Teaching and Practice

We can recognize every moment, every trigger, every experience as both a teaching and an opportunity for our practice of mindfulness and loving-kindness. That awareness is, all by itself, an empowering and liberating spiritual practice. It is also the basis for optimism. We come to see everything that happens to us from people and events as providing a path to awakening. I begin each day with the following daily affirmation that expresses this theme and inputs it as a spiritual resource to rely on:

I say Yes to everything that happens to me today
as an opportunity
to give and receive love without fear or
reserve.
I am thankful for the enduring capacity to love
that has come to me from the Sacred Heart of the
universe.
May everything that happens to me today
open my heart more and more.
May all that I think, say, feel, do, and am express
loving-kindness

toward myself, those close to me, and all beings.
May love be my life purpose, my bliss, my destiny,
  my calling,
the richest grace I can receive or give.
And may I always be especially compassionate
toward people who are considered least or last
or who feel alone or lost.

A Retreat

Going on a live-in retreat, especially a silent one, is an effective way of replenishing our inner resources. The fact that this happens in a spiritual setting is what makes it particularly valuable. We remove ourselves from our daily routine and reside in a place that respects our privacy and activates our discernment. We grow in self-trust when we sit with our deep questions, not forcing a reply but opening to any that might arise: Who are we now? Where do we go from here? How is the past a prologue? What does life ask of us now? What is ready to happen? What is ready to go? How can I be ready?

Evolutionary Consciousness

If my desire to awaken is, from a non-dual perspective, the urge of the universe itself to become self-aware, can we also say that it is the cosmic creative process that is rewiring its own brain?

—David R. Loy, *A New Buddhist Path*

We are evolution become intention. In evolution everything is arched toward transcending itself so it can become more than it is yet. In that sense it is spiritual. Since all is evolving, there is no endpoint. For instance, the oak tree I see outside my window is not in its final version of itself—nor will it ever be. It will continue to adjust itself to the changing conditions in the environment. It will continue to do what oaks have done for a thousand years, be more than they were a thousand years before. The same is true of us humans. We too are becoming more than we were in years past and even more than each of us was at birth. We are how the universe is rewiring itself. We are a future. So is what we call the higher power, as William Wordsworth says in "Outline": "universal earth / Dreaming on things to come."

"Entelechy" is a term from Aristotle. It refers to the inner drive, the lifelong principle that makes a living system be and act in accord with what it really is. A beaver builds a dam; a robin builds a nest; a human builds a house, family, society. Evolution is about how the entelechy of all beings and the universe itself continually activates itself so that we all keep moving toward our goal and purpose: oneness in commitment to building a world of justice, peace, and love. We can't help but open in this direction unless we put up a barrier against it. We can, however, stop or stunt our growth through addiction, greed, hate, division, ignorance, violence, revenge. Our only chance is the Dharma, the teachings about letting go of hate and practicing universal loving-kindness.

Our inner resources grow when we remain aware of our evolutionary nature and destiny. Then we understand the Buddhist teaching on impermanence: "I am not what I was in the past, I will not be what I am now for long. My goal is to embrace my rightful place in that ever-changing spectacle. My destiny is to become more than I ever dared imagine I could be. Then I will be a team member in the collective project of co-creating a society of justice, peace, and love." This is what is meant by an evolutionary spirituality. It is a powerful inner resource because we are ordaining ourselves as priests who are ever consecrating the world into the real presence of the divine. Likewise, when we devote ourselves to a larger destiny than our personal goals, we are animated by that bigness. Our hearts then *become* justice, peace, and love.

Finally, we sometimes wonder why we have the experience of impermanence—for example, by having continually altering moods, thoughts, feelings. Actually, impermanence is an evolutionary phenomenon; it is how change and progress happen: Everything is ever-changing in the universe, in science, in our brain in its neural plasticity. Relationships certainly change as conflicts intrude on romance. In fact, flowers given at romantic times are a subtle comment on impermanence. Yet, impermanence in nature also happens in reliable cycles of renewal, so impermanence does not have to mean a total ending after all. Seasons are hope's reply to impermanence.

Learning from the Symbolic Meaning of a Trigger

This book has shown us that as we take ownership of the triggers in our lives, they become resources. The triggering by others is now in our own hands. An actual trigger is part of a weapon. In the heroic journey story, the hero carries a weapon with which to fight the dragon or the enemy. The weapon takes on a symbolic meaning, just as the laser sword used by Luke Skywalker in the Star Wars saga is a symbol of his access to—and need for—spiritual resources. Often in myth we see the hero given a special weapon or talisman from a god or goddess, one designed specifically for the kind of enemy he will encounter.

Likewise, in Christian belief we are graced with special weapons to fight the forces of evil: "Therefore put on the full armor of God, so that when the day of evil comes, you may be able to stand your ground, and after you have done everything, be still standing. Stand firm then, with the belt of truth buckled around your waist, with the breastplate of righteousness in place (Ephesians 6:13–14). Thus, both in mythology and theology the weapon is a grace, a gift from a transcendent source, the unexpected inner resource, to help the hero fulfill his destiny. We can lose sight of a trigger as gift. We then become caught in combative energy, which moves us away from Source and inner resource. We lose touch with what William Wordsworth felt in "Tintern Abbey":

Our cheerful faith, that all which we behold
Is full of blessings.

The "monster," "dragon," or "enemy" is in reality an internal force, something primitive in us that opposes our higher rational, intelligent, and loving potentials. We might call this base element the part of the limbic system that is full of fear and reactiveness. Our inner resource comes from the other influence, the prefrontal cortex. As it manages our limbic responses, the whole system actually works as a resource.

Psychologically, triggers reveal our inner conflicts. Triggers show us exactly what is still awaiting resolution. Our inner resources help us toward the resolution. Thus, Luke holding the lightsaber, like Hercules holding his club, is not presenting two images, only one. The weapon reflects and portrays the direction of his life, the force of his purpose. If we can somehow find a way to interpret our triggers as revelations of our life purpose, we might appreciate them as resources in themselves. For instance, to be triggered by unfairness can become a calling to right wrongs not only for ourselves but for humanity as well.

When there is a similar theme in stories of all cultures, and one that endures through the centuries, we are seeing what people have taken to be a truth about *their own story and calling*. The characters, objects, and events of the "hero's journey" story, for instance, all reside in our collective psyche as energies awaiting activation.

We are not the superpower because we have the largest military on earth or because we have the strongest economy in the world. We should be a superpower because we espouse things that are important to everyone on earth.

—Jimmy Carter, Liberty University commencement speech,
Lynchburg, Virginia, 2018

The Power of Nature

Recognizing our oneness with nature is one form of freedom from dualism. Buddha's awakening happened when the morning star appeared. His first thought might have been "That star is not out there. It is I." We can even think of our meditative practices as joined to nature. From that oneness a path opens. The Zen master Shunryu Suzuki reminds us of this in *Not Always So*: "Although we practice with people, our goal is to practice with mountains and rivers, with trees and stones, with everything in the world, everything in the universe, and to find ourselves in this big cosmos. . . . [Then] we know intuitively which way to go." We move from practice to journey.

Spending time in nature, especially alone, creates and replenishes our spiritual resources. This happens because nature reflects our inner resources: We watch a sunrise and feel equipped to face what the day will bring, however daunting. We see a sunset and know we can let go of what is ending, however unwillingly. We experience the seasons and appreciate the phases of our lives, trusting that an irrepressible spring will follow the most defiantly prolonged winter. Daily time alone in the natural world—be it in a forest or by the ocean or simply under a tree—enlivens our resources. This is because we are part of nature, and acknowledging our connection arouses its power in us.

In his poem "Notes toward A Supreme Fiction," Wallace Stevens wrote, "Perhaps the truth depends upon a walk around the lake." These words mirror Psalm 85:11: "Truth shall spring out of the earth." Yes, we can find the truth, our truth, in the arms of Mother Nature. As our spiritual teacher she shows us the truth about the evolutionary impulse in us and in all things. Nature is transcendent because it yields a truth that transcends what our rational minds can conjure. Here is my poem:

It was when I beheld
The first cactus blossom
That all my questions
Went missing.
Gazing intently
Into the petals I
Found Dharma paradise, nothing
Left out.

EPILOGUE

THE FIRES THAT SHOW AND TELL

Scriptures [and teachings] are of little use to the enlightened person who sees the divine everywhere.
—*Bhagavad Gita*

Over the years I have meditated often on the following story from the Lotus Sutra, which expands on the preceding quotation, and I keep finding new realizations in it:

A father had gone to the market to buy, all he could afford, food for that night's supper. He returned from the market to find his house in fast-consuming flames. He was horrified to see his children in the windows laughing. Neighbors were calling to them, but they were refusing to come out. They were so fascinated by the colors and shapes of the flames that they wanted to stay in the blazing house, unaware of the peril. Realizing that they would soon perish, the father called to his children: "The toys you have been wanting, I brought them. So come out to get them!" At once the children ran out to safety *though their father had no toys at all.* They then thought they had been "taken for a ride," but it was only on the fastest chariot to enlightenment, disappointment in promises—which offers freedom from illusion, escape from the seductions that kill. What they did find were the genuine arms of loving-kindness, human connection, a life together—what really matters. We read in the poem by Francis Thompson, "The Hound of Heaven":

All which thy child's mistake
Fancies as lost, I have stored for thee at home:
    . . . clasp my hand and come!

In the story from the Lotus Sutra, the father was triggered by the sight of the children in the burning house and reacted with panic. His action was to call them to safety. The children were triggered by his promise and reacted by running out of the house.

This story is an allegory that can refer to our spirituality. We are the children. The house is our life and our story with all its absorbing, often illusory, yet seductively colorful dramas. The father is the Buddha, our great teacher. The father can also represent all the teachers and self-help writers we have learned from. The flames are the dramas themselves that we are caught up in, though they are dangerous. The toys are the teachings and practices that we imagine will give us all that we want, that will be a panacea for all our ills, that will make us feel good always. But nothing can do that. The "visions of sugar plums" that have "danced in our heads" do not find a match in reality.

All teachers and teachings are at their best when they lure us to the kind of safety we really need—though it is not as flashy as the colors and shapes of the dramas that attract us, so brimful of adrenaline. We find not a cure-all but only grounded reality that woos us from our habitual, housebound illusions. The be-all, end-all toys we might have hoped for are not really toys at all, only decoys. Yet, we need to fall for the decoys if we are ever to be liberated. This is the charming paradox about how we find the true teaching: which turns out to be nothing but yes to bare-bones reality shorn of every consoling and sheltering hideout.

The Buddha is the great trickster who has to say whatever it takes to save us from the house of our body-minds, on fire with triggers and reactions. The Dharma he offers is not as flashy as the toys we expected, but it provides freedom from fear and craving—

far more valuable than escape and comfort. The Dharma is shape-
less, but it grounds us on the bedrock of reality, far more precious
than any alluring fantasy our minds can conjure.

What will it take for each of us
To vacate all the tempting blaze
Of wily ghosts and mindmade dreams
That have so long enthralled our gaze
Not at what is but at what seems?

APPENDIX: AFFIRMATIONS TO FREE OURSELVES FROM THE GRIP OF FEAR

Use one or more of the following affirmations each day, repeating them often, feeling them bodily, and picturing yourself putting them into practice. Choose the ones that seem most appropriate for you. It also helps to read the ones you have chosen, or the whole list, onto your device and then listen to them each day. You then hear yourself sounding brave. Each affirmation becomes an exultant rap on the tambourine of freedom from fear.

- I trust my true fears to give me signals of real danger.
- I notice that I have unreal fears and worries.
- More and more I recognize the difference between real and imagined fears.
- I feel compassion toward myself for all the years I have been afraid.
- I forgive those who hypnotized me into unreal fears.
- I trust that I have as much fearlessness in me as fear.
- I trust the strength that opens in me when I have to face something.
- I believe in myself as able to handle whatever comes my way today.
- I create a pause between a trigger and my response.
- I have the inner resources to handle any fear or trigger.
- I find support inside and outside myself.
- I have an enormous capacity for rebuilding, restoring, and recovering from fear.
- I am more and more sure of my abilities.

- I am more and more aware of how I hold fear in my body.
- I relax the part of my body that holds my fear.
- I am freeing my body from the grip of fear.
- I open my body to joy and serenity.
- I let go of the stress and tension that come from fear.
- I let go of my fears of sickness, accidents, old age, and death.
- I let go of my fear of the future.
- I let go of regretful ties to the past.
- I let go of any tie I may still have to judgments my parents had of me.
- I let go of my fear of the unknown.
- I cease being afraid of knowing, having, or showing my feelings.
- I am less and less scared by what happens, by what has happened, by what will happen.
- I let go of my fear of what might happen.
- I let go of my obsessive thoughts about how the worst will happen.
- I let go of fear-based thoughts.
- I trust myself always to find a solution.
- I catch myself when I engage in paranoid fantasies and I let them go.
- My trust in myself is releasing me from fear and fearsome fantasies.
- I let go of regretting my mistakes; I find the path to going on.
- I let go of basing my decisions on fear.
- I let go of finding something to fear in everything.
- I let go of believing that everything is dangerous and headed for disaster.
- I see the humor in my exaggerated reactions to unreal dangers.
- I find a humorous response to every irrational fear.
- I smile at my scared ego and shrug off its relationship fears.
- I let go of my fear of aloneness or of time on my hands.

- I let go of my fear of abandonment.
- I let go of my fear of closeness.
- I let go of my fear of commitment.
- I let go of my fear of being vulnerable.
- I let go of my fear of giving or receiving.
- I let go of my fear of loving or being loved.
- I let go of believing I have to measure up to what others want me to be.
- I give up having to be perfect.
- I let go of my performance fears.
- I let go of my sexual fears.
- I advocate for myself and notice my courage widening and deepening.
- I am confident in my ability to deal with people or situations that scare me.
- I let go of my fear of any person.
- I let go of my fear of saying no to others.
- I let go of my fear of saying yes.
- I cease being intimidated by others' anger.
- I give up trying to appease those who intimidate me.
- Attempts to bully me now fall flat.
- I let go of being on the defensive.
- I protect myself while always being committed to nonviolence.
- I stick to my guns and I hold my fire.
- I let go of feeling obliged to do things his (or her, or their) way.
- I let go of the need to meet others' expectations.
- I state and protect my personal boundaries.
- I let go of my fear of what might happen if people dislike me.
- I let go of my terror about disapproval, ridicule, exclusion, or rejection.
- I dare to stop auditioning for people's approval or love.
- I give up the need to correct people's impressions of me.
- I give up my poses, pretenses, and posturings; I dare to be myself.

- I dare to show my hand, to show my passions, to show my enthusiasms, to show my real feelings, longings, and needs.
- I want my every word, feeling, and deed to reveal me as I truly am.
- I give up being afraid of what I want.
- I ask for what I want.
- I love being found out, caught in the act of being my authentic self.
- I dare to live the life that truly reflects my deepest needs and wishes.
- I let go of my fear of spending, saving, sharing money.
- I let go of the fear that I will lose, lose face, lose freedom, lose friends, lose family members, lose respect, lose status, lose my job, lose out.
- I let go of my fear of having to grieve.
- I let go of fears about my adequacy as a parent or child, partner or friend.
- I let go of my fear of the fearsome givens of life: impermanence, change, suffering, unfairness, failed plans, losses, and betrayals.
- I am flexible enough to accept life as it is.
- I am forgiving enough to accept how I have lived my life so far.
- I trust my present predicament as a path.
- I let go of control; I let the chips fall where they may.
- I let go of more than any fate can take away from me.
- I cease being afraid of my own power.
- I cease being afraid of the power of others.
- I let go of my fear of authority.
- I speak truth to power.
- I dare to take a stand for the oppressed and the marginalized.
- I join with the most vulnerable in our society.
- I dare to devote my life to co-creating a world of justice, peace, and love.

- As I show courage for social justice, I notice I am letting go of fear in all areas of my life.
- I have pluck and wit.
- I meet danger face-to-face.
- I stand up to a fight.
- I speak up for myself.
- I speak up for others.
- I trust ever-renewing sources of bravery within me.
- I let go of having any fear stop or drive me.
- Nothing forces me; nothing holds me back.
- I am a hero: I live through pain and am transformed by it.
- I show grace under pressure.
- I stop running; I stop hiding.
- I let go of hesitation and self-doubt.
- I notice primitive dreads in me—for example, that if I love something I will lose it or have it taken away from me; that if something is good it won't last; that if something is bad it will get worse. I recognize these beliefs as superstitions and let go of the fears that support them.
- I take risks and yet I act with responsibility and caring.
- I keep finding alternatives behind the apparent dead-end of fear.
- I let go of scanning my life to find a reason to be afraid.
- I give up my need to find something to fear.
- More and more my fear is becoming healthy excitement.
- I let fear go and let joy in.
- I let fear go and let love in.
- I am grateful for the love that awaits me everywhere.
- I know I am deeply loved by many people near and far.
- I feel lovingly held by a higher power (God, Universe, Buddha, etc.).
- As I devote myself more and more to a higher power than myself I feel it alive through, with, and in me.

- I believe that I have an important destiny and that I am living in accord with it.
- I am more and more aware of others' fears, more and more sensitive to them, more and more compassionate toward them.
- I enlarge my circle of love to include every living being.
- I keep finding ways to show my love.
- I am great-hearted and bold-spirited.
- I let go of ill will toward those who have hurt me.
- I do good to those who hate me, bless those who curse me, pray or wish enlightenment for those who have mistreated me.
- I can say "Ouch!" and open a dialogue rather than retaliate.
- I dare to give of myself unconditionally and I dare to be unconditionally committed to maintaining my own boundaries.
- I honor and evoke my animal powers, my human powers, my divine powers.
- I set free my love, until now imprisoned by fear.
- I set free my joy, until now inhibited by fear.
- I let true love cast out fear.
- May I always choose the path of gentle love, the best antidote to fear.
- I say yes to all that happens to me today as an opportunity to love more and fear less.
- I keep letting go and I keep going on.
- I feel an enduring fearlessness awakening in me.
- I keep affirming my freedom from fear.
- I am thankful for the grace of finding freedom from fear.
- May all beings find freedom from fear.

The certainty that nothing can happen to us that does not belong to us in our innermost being is the foundation of . . . fearlessness . . . Then life has lost its horrors and suffering its sting.

—Lama Anagarika Govinda, *Foundations of Tibetan Mysticism*

ABOUT THE AUTHOR

David Richo, PhD, MFT, is a psychotherapist and workshop leader who lives in Santa Barbara and San Francisco, California. He combines Jungian, Buddhist, and mythic perspectives in his work. Dave is the author of the following books:

How to Be an Adult: A Handbook on Psychological and Spiritual Integration (Paulist Press, 1991)
Happy, mature people have somehow picked up the knack of being generous with their sympathies while still taking care of themselves. We can all evolve from the neurotic ego through a healthy ego to the spiritual Self. We can deal with fear, anger, and guilt. We can be assertive, have boundaries, and build intimacy.

When Love Meets Fear: How to Become Defense-less and Resource-full (Paulist Press, 1997)
Our lively energy is inhibited by fear and we are so often needlessly on the defensive. We consider the origins and healings of our fears of closeness, commitment, aloneness, assertiveness, and panic attacks. We can free ourselves from the grip of fear so that it no longer stops or drives us.

Shadow Dance: Liberating the Power and Creativity of Your Dark Side (Shambhala Publications, 1999)
The shadow is all that we abhor about ourselves as well as all the dazzling potential that we doubt or deny we have. We project these onto others as dislike or admiration. We can acknowledge our limitations and our gifts. Then both our light and dark sides become sources of creativity and grant us access to our untapped inner wealth.

How to Be an Adult in Relationships: The Five Keys to Mindful Loving (Shambhala Publications, 2002)
Love is not so much a feeling as a way of being present. Love is presence with these five *A*s: unconditional attention, acceptance, appreciation, affection, and allowing others to be as they are. Love is presence without the five conditioned overlays of ego: judgment, fear, control, attachment, and illusion.

The Five Things We Cannot Change and the Happiness We Find by Embracing Them (Shambhala Publications, 2005)
There are unavoidable "givens" in life and relationships. By our unconditional yes to these conditions of existence we learn to open, accept, even embrace our predicaments without trying to control the outcomes. We begin to trust what happens as gifts of grace that help us grow in character, depth, and compassion.

The Power of Coincidence: How Life Shows Us What We Need to Know (Shambhala Publications, 2007)
There are meaningful coincidences of events, dreams, or relationships that happen to us beyond our control. These synchronicities influence the course of our life in mysterious ways. They often reveal assisting forces that are pointing us to our unguessed, unexpected, and unimagined destiny.

The Sacred Heart of the World: Restoring Mystical Devotion to Our Spiritual Life (Paulist Press, 2007)
We explore the symbolism of the heart in world religious traditions, and then trace the historical thread of Christian devotion to the Sacred Heart of Jesus into modern times. We focus on the philosophy and theology of Teilhard de Chardin and Karl Rahner to design a new sense of what devotion can be.

Making Love Last: How to Sustain Intimacy and Nurture Connection (set of 3 CDs; Shambhala Publications, 2008)
Recording from a lively workshop given by David Richo at Spirit Rock Buddhist Retreat Center in California on relationship is-

sues. Topics include how love can endure, fears of intimacy and commitment, trust and fidelity, resolving our conflicts, the phases of a relationship, and how our early life affects our adult relationships.

When the Past Is Present: Healing the Emotional Wounds That Sabotage Our Relationships (Shambhala Publications, 2008)
Transference is a tendency to see our parents or other significant characters in our life story in others. In this book, we explore how our past impacts our present relationships. We find ways to make transference a valuable opportunity to learn about ourselves, deepen our relationships, and heal our ancient wounds.

Being True to Life: Poetic Paths to Personal Growth (Shambhala Publications, 2009)
Poetry may have seemed daunting in school but here is a chance for it to become quite wonderfully personal and spiritually enriching. This book offers an opportunity to use our hearts and pens to release the full range of our imagination to discover ourselves through reading and writing poetry.

Daring to Trust: Opening Ourselves to Real Love and Intimacy (Shambhala Publications, 2010)
We learn how to build trust, how to recognize a trustworthy person, how to work with our fears around trusting, and how to rebuild trust after a breach or infidelity. We find ways to trust others, to trust ourselves, to trust reality and the events that happen to us, and to trust a higher power than ourselves.

How to Be an Adult in Faith and Spirituality (Paulist Press, 2011)
We explore and compare religion and spirituality with an emphasis on how they can both become rich resources for personal growth. We increase our understanding of God, faith, and life's plaguing questions in the light of mysticism, depth psychology, and our new appreciation of evolutionary cosmology.

How to Be an Adult in Faith and Spirituality
(set of 4 CDs; Paulist Press, 2012)
Recording from a workshop given at Spirit Rock Buddhist Retreat Center in California on how to design and practice an adult spirituality. We also look at how to find the spiritual riches in religion while letting go of the elements of religion that are not in keeping with our adult evolution.

Coming Home to Who You Are: Discovering Your Natural Capacity for Love, Integrity, and Compassion
(Shambhala Publications, 2011)
This book offers practices that can usher us into a new way of being alive—as cheerful agents of the goodness that is in us all. Our choices for integrity and loving-kindness reflect that goodness and help us co-create a world of justice, peace, and love. This is an owners' guide to being an upright and loving human.

Embracing the Shadow: Discovering the Hidden Riches in Our Relationships (set of 4 CDs Shambhala Publications, 2013)
This recording of a live presentation addresses working with our unskillful tendencies in our relationships so that we can tame them and grow because of them. We notice our projections onto one another. We find the gifts we might not yet have dared to recognize or show. We learn how working with the dark rather than in it lets the light of intimacy through.

How to Be an Adult in Relationships
(audiobook, read by the author; Shambhala Publications, 2013)

How to Be an Adult in Love: Letting Love in Safely and Showing It Recklessly (Shambhala Publications, 2013)
Love is what we were born to show and receive. Yet, we sometimes fear giving or receiving it. This book helps us learn to love ourselves, partners, others, and the human family while finding ways to let go of fear, ego-centeredness, and the will to revenge.

Everyone can practice loving-kindness in ways that make love unconditional, universal, and joyful too.

The Power of Grace: Recognizing Unexpected Gifts on the Path (Shambhala Publications, 2014)
Personal growth involves more than applying ourselves to self-help or spiritual practices. Somewhere in the episodes and milestones of our lives something positive or life-changing happened, something beneficial, that was beyond our effort, plan, or expectation. That special assistance—unmerited, unearned, unplanned, often unnoticed—is called grace, the amazing gift dimension of life.

When Catholic Means Cosmic: Opening to a Big-Minded, Big-Hearted Faith (Paulist Press, 2015)
When the Catholic faith has cosmic dimensions, we and our religion expand: We update our beliefs in accord with the best advances in psychology and science. We maintain and appreciate the riches of our religion while being contemporary too. People of all traditions will find this book helpful in the way it explores how religion and spirituality can be integrated.

You Are Not What You Think: The Egoless Path to Self-Esteem and Generous Love (Shambhala Publications, 2015)
We can look at the "big ego" in ourselves and others not with disdain but with compassion. We can tame our own ego so that it becomes healthy and ready for relationships, both in partnering and at home and work. We find practices that help us let go of ego-centeredness and move toward self-esteem and spiritual progress.

When Mary Becomes Cosmic: A Jungian and Mystical Path to the Divine Feminine (Paulist Press, 2016)
Our vision of Mary can become cosmic in scope. The Jungian archetype of the divine feminine as personified by Mary is built into the design of every human psyche. Her ancient titles reflect the

marvelous qualities of our own essential Self and Mother Earth. Every religious truth and image is a metaphor for who we and the world are.

The Five Longings: What We've Always Wanted and Already Have (Shambhala Publications, 2017)
There are five longings deep within us: to love and be loved, to find meaning in life and to have a meaningful life, to be free to be ourselves fully without restraint or inhibition, to find true happiness and serenity, and to keep growing psychologically and spiritually. We explore each of these to find out who we really are.

Everything Ablaze: Meditating on the Mystical Vision of Teilhard de Chardin (Paulist Press, 2017)
Contemporary interest in Teilhard de Chardin's work manifests the evolutionary mysticism he taught and forecast, and which we can apply to our daily life. This is conscious evolution, a presence in the world as members of Christ's body. Then we co-create the future of justice, peace, and love that Christ came to proclaim.

Five True Things: A Little Guide to Embracing Life's Big Challenges (Shambhala Publications, 2019)
A revised and abridged version of *The Five Things We Cannot Change and the Happiness We Find by Embracing Them.*

For more information, upcoming events, and a catalog of audio programs, visit davericho.com.